History Makers

Isaac
Newton

Scientist

Andrew May

Cavendish Square

New York

Published in 2017 by Cavendish Square Publishing, LLC
243 5th Avenue, Suite 136, New York, NY 10016

Library of Congress Cataloging-in-Publication Data

Names: May, Andrew, author.
Title: Isaac Newton: Scientist / Andrew May.
Description: New York : Cavendish Square Publishing, [2017] |
Series: History makers | Includes bibliographical references and index.
Identifiers: LCCN 2016011481 (print) | LCCN 2016012128 (ebook) |
ISBN 9781502619228 (library bound) | ISBN 9781502619235 (ebook)
Subjects: LCSH: Newton, Isaac, 1642-1727. | Physicists--Great Britain--Biography. |
Mathematicians--Great Britain--Biography. | Physics--History.
Classification: LCC QC16 .N7 M3745 2017 (print) | LCC QC16 .N7 (ebook) | DDC 530.092--dc23
LC record available at http://lccn.loc.gov/2016011481

Editorial Director: David McNamara
Editor: Renni Johnson
Copy Editor: Michele Suchomel-Casey
Art Director: Jeffrey Talbot
Designer: Jessica Nevins
Production Assistant: Karol Szymczuk
Photo Research: J8 Media

Printed in the United States of America

Table of Contents

1 The Newtonian Universe

The world has changed beyond recognition since Isaac Newton's time. Feats of engineering that we now take for granted would have been unimaginable three centuries ago: skyscrapers, ocean liners, supersonic aircraft, artificial satellites, interplanetary space probes... And the methods employed by designers today would have seemed strange and magical to a person of the seventeenth century, for the process starts with the writing down of symbols on a piece of paper (or, these days, on a computer screen)—precise mathematical

Isaac Newton developed calculus and studied the phenomenon of gravity.

equations describing the forces, motions, and interactions involved. In the realm of modern engineering, everything has a symbolic life before it takes on a real, material existence.

The same principle extends far beyond man-made technology. Bizarre and improbable as it may seem on the face of it, everything in the physical universe obeys strict mathematical rules. At the start of the seventeenth century, no one would have believed that. By the end of the eighteenth century, however, virtually everyone did so. The man who persuaded the world to change its mind was Isaac Newton.

When Newton started his studies, universities throughout Europe were still teaching Aristotle's system of **natural philosophy** as the standard picture of the physical world. Aristotle's theory had no symbols or equations in it. Some of the pre-**Aristotelian** Greek philosophers—notably Pythagoras and his followers—did believe in a fundamentally mathematical world, but over time their views had fallen out of favor. More often than not such ideas were dismissed as the musings of crackpots or mystical dreamers. A similar attitude prevailed toward the **Hermetic** philosophers of medieval Europe—a small and secretive minority who believed that, with sufficient diligence, it would be possible to discover a simple set of rules capable of explaining the complexities of the natural world.

The situation in Newton's time was, in a sense, the mirror image of the present day. What then seemed to be a bizarre and mystical notion—that the universe obeys simple mathematical laws—is now seen as the "rational" view. But in those days, "rational" people tended to assume the exact opposite. The world looked complex, chaotic, and unpredictable…so clearly it could have nothing to do with the simplicity of mathematics.

When Newton published his greatest masterpiece in 1687, he called it *Philosophiae Naturalis Principia Mathematica*—"Mathematical Principles of Natural Philosophy." The book was a revolution, and the essence of that revolution is summed up in the title. Before 1687, "mathematical principles" and "natural philosophy" were two completely different branches of knowledge, poles apart. After *Principia* they would be tied together by a bond that could never be broken.

Today, as an academic discipline, "theoretical physics" is virtually synonymous with "**applied mathematics**." You cannot study either subject without seeing Newton's influence at every turn. He discovered the **law of gravity** and codified the laws of motion. He developed pioneering methods in mathematics. He invented a new kind of telescope and brought new insights to the analysis of optical phenomena. Science has continued to advance since Newton's time, but it has done so by building on his work, not by sweeping it aside. For all the scientific revolutions of later centuries, the world continues to obey the basic mathematical laws discovered by Newton. There is no disputing the fact that we live in a **Newtonian** universe.

Was this the goal that Newton was working toward? Did he have a prophetic vision of modern science that he pursued single-mindedly throughout his life? Was it his intention to transform human understanding?

The answer is almost certainly "no." All the towering accomplishments for which Newton is remembered were made in a few short bursts, dotted among countless other studies—theology, **alchemy**, ancient history—that are now all but forgotten. On the few occasions Newton could be persuaded to publish his scientific work, he did so with obvious reluctance. Science, in the modern sense of the word, was just one small aspect of what inspired him.

This fact was carefully swept under the rug for two hundred years. Throughout the eighteenth and nineteenth centuries, historians focused on Newton's scientific achievements to the virtual exclusion of everything else. It is only in the last hundred years or so that some people—and still only a minority—have made an effort to understand Newton as something other than a "modern" scientist. A prominent figure in this context was John Maynard Keynes, a man best known as one of the twentieth century's leading economists. During the 1930s, he became increasingly interested in Newton's life and purchased a number of his unpublished private papers.

The papers Keynes acquired were ones that did not interest the academic institutions of the day, dealing as they did with "unimportant" subjects such as alchemy and religion. Yet it is these very writings that give the clearest insight into Newton's personality and motivation. Through them it becomes clear that his scientific and "non-scientific" activities were all part of the same basic quest. As Keynes wrote: "He looked on the whole universe and all that is in it as a riddle, as a secret which could be read by applying pure thought to certain evidence, certain mystic clues which God had laid about the world."

Horrifying as it may sound to modern scientists, Isaac Newton was a Creationist. He believed that God had made the universe according to a precise and rational design. He also believed that the details of this design had been fully revealed to the people of the earliest civilizations. In other words, just like the New Agers of today, Newton was a believer in ancient wisdom—*prisca sapientia*, as it was known in Latin. He believed that over the course of time this primal knowledge had been lost, and he considered it his life's work to rediscover it. His study of mathematics and natural philosophy formed part of this quest, but so did his alchemical and biblical researches. To Newton, all these activities were equally important.

Like the medieval Hermeticists before him, Newton believed there were ancient secrets hidden in cryptic documents or encoded in the very structure of the universe, waiting to be unlocked. To quote Keynes again:

> *He believed that these clues were to be found partly in the evidence of the heavens and in the constitution of elements ... but also partly in certain papers and traditions handed down by the brethren in*

an unbroken chain back to the original cryptic
revelation in Babylonia. He regarded the universe
as a cryptogram set by the Almighty.

One of the most important principles of Hermetic philosophy is enshrined in the maxim, "As above, so below." In other words, there is a correspondence between the familiar world of human experience and the universe on a cosmic scale. It was a principle Newton took to heart. It infused everything he turned his mind to, from alchemy and the chronology of ancient kingdoms to the mathematical principles of natural philosophy.

It is difficult to avoid the conclusion that Newton's greatest scientific and mathematical achievement—the foundation stone of modern rational science—was the fruit of a broader project that today would be dismissed as mystical nonsense. To Newton, mathematics was nothing less than the language of God. As confirmation of this, he cited the Wisdom of Solomon 11:20: "Thou hast ordered all things in measure and number and weight." Just like the Christian fundamentalists whom modern scientists consider to be their arch opponents, Newton looked to the Bible as the ultimate authority in all things.

To Newton, science was not about discovery so much as rediscovery. He was convinced the Ancients had known everything there was to know and that so-called modern insights were simply sweeping away the ignorance and false views that had accumulated in the intervening years. Even the great revolution of Copernicus and Galileo, putting the sun rather than Earth

The writings of Hermes Trismegistus influenced
medieval alchemists and led to the Hermetic movement
in western Europe.

Isaac Newton (*seated*), circa 1880, served as president of the Royal Society of London for Improving Natural Knowledge.

at the center of the planetary system, was—to Newton's way of thinking—nothing new. In his own words: "It was the most ancient opinion that the planets revolved about the Sun; that the Earth, as one of the planets, described an annual course about the Sun, while by a diurnal motion it turned on its axis, and that the Sun remained at rest."

Taken in isolation from his accomplishments, it would be easy to dismiss Newton's world view on the grounds that countless astrologers, alchemists, Hermeticists, and New Agers have held similar views before and since. But Newton was unique. He succeeded where so many others have failed. He discovered a symbolic code—applied mathematics—*that actually works*. He showed that the ancient maxim—as above, so below—was nothing short of the truth. When his mathematical code was superimposed on the real world it turned out to have a predictive power the like of which had never been seen before. Newton's approach—applying "mathematical principles" to "natural philosophy"—revolutionized how scientists think about the physical universe. It paved the way for the high-tech world in which we live today.

2

On the Shoulders of Giants

If I have seen further it is by standing on the shoulders of giants.

Isaac Newton,
letter to Robert Hooke

Newton's research wasn't carried out in isolation. He read the work of his predecessors, and he corresponded with his contemporaries. Among the latter was Robert Hooke (1635–1703), who was destined to become his scientific *bête noire*. In a letter to Hooke in 1676, Newton wrote, "If I have seen further it is by standing on the shoulders of giants." In other words, Newton was simply building on the work of others who had gone before him. (This is even true of the "shoulders

This engraving depicts Isaac Newton's quarters at Trinity College, Cambridge.

of giants" metaphor itself. Although it is often believed to be Newton's invention, he was merely paraphrasing a popular saying of the time: "a dwarf standing on the shoulders of a giant may see farther than a giant himself.")

For Newton, it was quite an effort to clamber onto the shoulders of the giants who had preceded him. He was born with no great prospects in the winter of 1642—on Christmas Day, according to the Old Style calendar then in use in England. This was a time of great turmoil: the civil war between Parliament and Charles I had begun just two months earlier, with the Battle of Edgehill. The war and the interregnum that followed dominated English politics during the first seventeen years of Newton's life.

Newton's birthplace was Woolsthorpe Manor (despite its grand-sounding name, the "manor" was nothing more than a modest farmhouse) near Grantham in rural Lincolnshire. Newton's father died shortly before Isaac was born, and his mother moved out of the house three years later when she married the rector of a neighboring village. The house and farm, together with Isaac, were left in the care of his paternal grandparents until his mother returned to Woolsthorpe after the death of her second husband in 1653. To the dismay of eleven-year-old Isaac, she brought three young children with her—a new half brother and two half sisters.

The following year Isaac's mother sent him to the King's School in Grantham, some seven or so miles (11 kilometers) away. This was too far to walk each day, so he lodged in the town with an apothecary named William Clark. For young Isaac, this provided a much more stimulating environment than anything he had known previously. It may have helped to spark his interest in science—it certainly gave him access to a more interesting selection of books than the standard school curriculum of Latin and theology.

There aren't many anecdotes from Newton's childhood—and those that survive may be apocryphal since they were written down decades later, after he had become famous. The general picture is of a youngster who was far from being top of his class in school, yet was remarkably inventive outside it. The teenage Isaac spent his leisure hours building mechanical devices such as kites, windmills, water clocks, and even toys for his younger siblings. He seems to have enjoyed novelty and hated routine.

According to one of Newton's early biographers, "He invented the trick of a paper lantern with a candle in it, tied to the tail of a kite. This wonderfully affrighted all the neighboring inhabitants for some time." Presumably such escapades took place at night, when it is easy to imagine the consternation that a flickering light hovering in midair might cause. A mischievous teenager wishing to create his own "UFO scare" could scarcely do better today!

Toward the end of 1659, when Newton was approaching seventeen, his mother decided it was time for him to start running the farm. That was the last thing the restless, imaginative, inventive youth wanted to do. By all accounts, he tried his best to carry out his duties as incompetently as possible. There is even a court record testifying to the fact that young Mr. Newton was fined "for allowing his swine to trespass and his fences to lie in disrepair."

Fortunately, escape was at hand. Newton's mother had a brother who proved to be more sympathetic toward the budding scientist. The Reverend William Ayscough had studied at Trinity College in Cambridge and could see his nephew's scholarly promise. With the support of his headmaster, Newton was sent off to Trinity in June 1661.

Cambridge was one of only two university towns in England at this time. Closer and hence more convenient than Oxford, it was still 60 miles (96.6 km) from Woolsthorpe, more than a day's journey away. Like Oxford, Cambridge was organized on a collegiate system, Trinity College being one of sixteen making up Cambridge University. Newton entered it as the lowest grade of student, a subsizar, which meant he had to pay his way by acting as a servant to other, richer students.

"Science" wasn't a recognized subject of study in the seventeenth century. The word existed, but it had the same broad meaning—of knowledge in any discipline—as its Latin root *scientia*. Analysis of the physical world was considered to be a branch of philosophy, just as it had been in ancient Greece. What we would today describe as "science" was then called "natural philosophy." In his writings Newton often refers simply to "philosophy" since natural philosophy was the only kind of philosophy with which he was concerned.

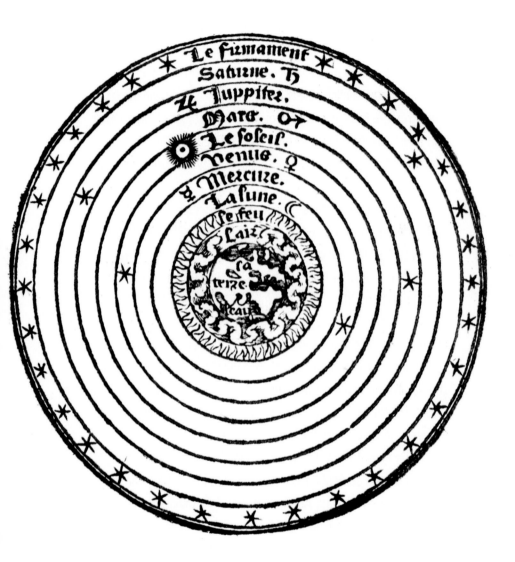

Aristotle's geocentric model of the solar system, depicting Earth at the center, surrounded by the moon, sun, and planets, was taught at Cambridge when Newton was an undergraduate.

For centuries, Aristotle (384–322 BCE) had been considered the supreme authority on the subject of natural philosophy. His teachings were seen as being consistent with, and complementary to, the Judeo-Christian beliefs that underpinned European medieval thought. The Bible is rather vague on the subject of what today would be called physics, so the copious writings of Aristotle were used to fill the gaps, and Aristotle's work was taught with the same dogmatic zeal as the Old Testament.

It was one of Aristotle's fundamental principles that different sets of rules applied on Earth and in the heavens, the dividing line being just inside the orbit of the moon. On Earth, for example, it is in the nature of moving objects to slow down and come to rest. Everything this side of the moon is subject to gravity, which is the natural tendency of heavy objects to fall downward—the heavier the object, the faster the rate of fall. On the other hand, the natural form of motion in the heavens is a circle. All celestial bodies rotate around Earth on perfectly circular orbits, for all eternity. (Warning to the reader: Every statement from Aristotle above is incorrect. Aristotle was wrong!)

When Newton arrived in Cambridge, Aristotle dominated the undergraduate curriculum. Students were taught Aristotelian logic, Aristotelian ethics, and Aristotelian natural philosophy. Newton was less than impressed—he didn't bother to finish reading any of the set texts. In his undergraduate notebook, he wrote "amicus Aristoteles magis amica veritas," meaning "Aristotle is my friend but a greater friend is Truth."

Physicist and astronomer Galileo Galilei was a proponent
of a planetary system that put the sun at the center. Newton
valued Galileo's views over Aristotle's.

Newton therefore turned his attention to more recent writings of his own choosing—works by the likes of Galileo Galilei, Johannes Kepler, René Descartes, and Francis Bacon.

Galileo (1564–1642), who died the year Newton was born, was a fervent anti-Aristotelian. He promoted the idea of a sun-centered planetary system, originally proposed by Copernicus (1473–1543) in the sixteenth century, in direct opposition to Aristotle's Earth-centered view. Unlike Aristotle, whose assertions were all based on supposed "common sense," Galileo made observations and carried out experiments. He used a telescope to show that Jupiter's moons orbited the planet like a miniature solar system. He conducted experiments with falling bodies and inclined planes in order to refute long-standing Aristotelian misconceptions about gravity and to demonstrate concepts such as acceleration and inertia, which are indispensable to a proper understanding of the physics of motion.

The German astronomer Johannes Kepler (1571–1630) was a near-contemporary of Galileo. He outlined three laws of planetary motion, which went on to play an important role in Newton's formulation of the law of gravity. Although the same word, "law," is used in both cases, it is not employed in quite the same sense. Newton's law of gravity is a fully worked-out mathematical theory that describes how a certain type of force operates. Kepler's laws, on the other hand, constitute an empirical description of the way planets move around the sun, without saying anything about the forces involved or their underlying principles.

The three laws of planetary motion outlined by Johannes Kepler, German mathematician and astronomer, would influence Newton's law of gravity.

Kepler's first law was possibly the most revolutionary of the three because it was the first time that anyone had suggested that planets move in anything other than circular orbits. A circle is the shape you get if the distance from the planet to the center of rotation always remains constant. But what if there are two "centers," slightly offset from each other? If the average distance between the planet and each "center"—or focus, to use the correct word—remains constant, then the resulting oval shape is called an ellipse. According to Kepler's first law, the planets move on elliptical orbits with the sun at one focus (the other focus is "empty").

Kepler's second and third laws are numerical, based on careful observation of the rate at which planets move around their elliptical orbits. The second law states that a planet sweeps out equal-area segments of the ellipse in equal periods of time. The third law, which is the most mathematical, states that the square of the orbital period is proportional to the cube of the longest dimension of the ellipse. Taken together, the three laws provide a complete description of planetary motion.

By Newton's time, thanks to the work of people such as Galileo and Kepler, a modern picture of the universe was beginning to emerge. Regardless of the Aristotelian orthodoxy still being purveyed by university lecturers, there were those who had come to realize that the stars were in fact other suns spread throughout space and that Earth was just another planet.

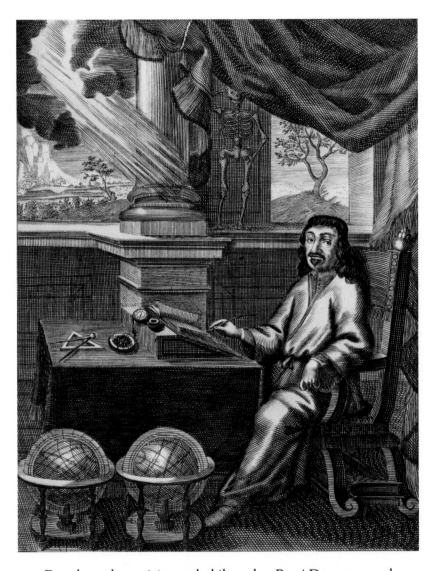

French mathematician and philosopher René Descartes used math to explain natural science.

In his letter to Hooke about the shoulders of giants, Newton specifically refers to the French philosopher René Descartes (1596–1650). Galileo and Kepler had described *how* planets move. Descartes went a step further and asked *why* they move like that. Descartes was a mathematician as well as a philosopher, but in his day—before Newton, in other words—there was no such thing as applied mathematics. People were happy to use mathematical formulae to *describe* nature, as in the case of Kepler's laws, but it never occurred to anyone to use them to *explain* nature. So when Descartes turned his attention to the question of why planets move in accordance with Kepler's laws, the explanation he came up with was qualitative rather than quantitative.

Descartes was a pioneer of what became known as the "mechanical" view of the universe, according to which bodies can only interact with each other through physical contact. Any suggestion of "action at a distance" was anathema to this view—a throwback to the superstition and mysticism of the past. In order to reconcile observed orbital motions with his mechanistic philosophy, Descartes proposed a theory in which the planets are swept around the sun by rotating vortices of invisible particles. By Newton's time this had become the accepted model of planetary motion.

Sir Francis Bacon (1561–1626) was an English near-contemporary of Galileo. Like his Italian counterpart, he was an outspoken opponent of Aristotle. He believed that the way to the truth lay through experiment and observation, rather than

Francis Bacon, circa 1738, also valued science and evidence over Aristotelian logic.

through (potentially flawed) reasoning. Aristotle had laid out his rules of strict deductive logic in a work called the *Organon*, but Bacon believed Aristotle's approach was inadequate to the task of making sense of the real world. In 1620 he wrote a work of his own, called *The New Organon*, in which he proposed a powerful alternative to Aristotelian deduction. Bacon called this new process "induction," and it soon became known as the Baconian method in his honor. These days, people simply call it the **scientific method**.

Francis Bacon was an influential figure in the social circles of his day, and his preoccupation with experimental science meant that it suddenly became a fashionable pastime among the English gentry. Eventually this led to the creation of an organization devoted specifically to this activity: the Royal Society of London for Improving Natural Knowledge. Founded in 1663, the Royal Society's stated aim was to promote and disseminate "experimental philosophy." In defiance of the dogmatic teaching of Aristotle in universities throughout Europe, the society adopted the motto *Nullius in verba*—loosely translated as "nothing by authority" or "take no-one's word for it."

There was another strand to the intellectual world of Newton's time. While the teachings of Aristotle were broadcast in university lecture theatres, and groups like the Royal Society held meetings that were open to the public, other seekers after truth pursued their research in private and guarded their secrets jealously. These were the disciples of the Hermetic tradition, striving after what was termed "**occult**" knowledge. To them, "occult" retained its original meaning of hidden or secret, but to outsiders it had already acquired its modern meaning of "mystical" or "supernatural"— usually intended as a pejorative. Galileo, for example, objected to the now-accepted theory that the moon causes Earth's tides on the grounds that it was "occult."

Newton was attracted to the occult in its original sense. He seems to have been a naturally secretive person—he often wrote in code, for example—who was perfectly happy conducting research for his own benefit and no one else's. But the idea of secrecy was anathema to the spirit of the Royal Society. Its members were keen to see their work broadcast as widely as possible. In the early years this was achieved by means of letters circulated by the secretary, Henry Oldenburg (1619–1677), who acted as the central focus for interchange between dozens of researchers all across Britain and Europe. Then in 1665, the first English-language journal of science made its appearance: *Philosophical Transactions of the Royal Society*, with Oldenburg as editor.

Eventually Newton would find himself drawn, not entirely willingly, into the world of the Royal Society. Before then he had some major scientific discoveries to make—and he made them on his own, in secret.

3

The Most Famous Apple in History

The life of a Cambridge academic suited Newton perfectly. When he graduated in 1665 he would have liked nothing better than to stay on at Trinity to continue the various lines of research he had begun. Fate intervened, however—1665 was the year of the Great Plague.

Although the plague was centered on London, Cambridge was considered close enough—and densely populated enough—to be at risk. As a precautionary measure the university was closed down and the students sent home until the threat of contagion

An artistic rendering, circa 1880, of Isaac Newton seeing the apple fall and developing his first theories about gravity had receded. It seems unlikely, students being students, that many of them chose to take their work home with them. But one of them did.

As soon as Newton arrived back at Woolsthorpe, he turned his attention to a number of problems he had started to think about in his final undergraduate year. He worked on them, in a creative frenzy, for the entire duration of his enforced leave. Historians often refer to this period as Newton's *annus mirabilis* ("remarkable year") although it was actually closer to eighteen months before he finally returned to Cambridge, early in 1667.

During this remarkably productive time, Newton developed new techniques in pure mathematics, including the generalized **binomial theorem**, which is one of the most powerful formulae in algebra. He also carried out a number of pioneering optical experiments, such as his famous experiment with a prism that showed for the first time that white light is made up of all the colors of the spectrum. Previously—all the way back to Aristotle—it had been assumed that white light was "pure" and that color was something that had to be added to it.

The topic Newton grappled with most at Woolsthorpe was gravity. He began by considering the motion of the moon. The problem that bothered him was not *how* the moon moves but *why*. To Aristotle, the answer was simple: a circular orbit centered on Earth was the "natural motion" in the heavens, just as falling vertically downward was the "natural motion" for Earth-bound objects. But in the new post-Copernican, post-Galilean universe the situation was more complicated. Earth orbits around the sun. The other planets also orbit around the sun. The moon orbits around Earth. The satellites of Jupiter, which Galileo had observed through his telescope, orbit around Jupiter. There is no longer a single center around which all heavenly bodies revolve and toward which all mundane objects fall. Everywhere Newton looked, he could see problems people had never considered before. How do things fall on other planets? Why doesn't the moon fall to Earth? What prevents Jupiter's satellites from drifting away from their parent planet?

We now know that the key to all these mysteries is gravity. Newton seems to have grasped this intuitively at a very early stage in his musings. But proving it to his own satisfaction— and working out all the details—was another matter altogether. "I began to think of gravity extending to the orb of the Moon," Newton wrote much later about this period of his life. He knew that gravity was a force acting on material objects, and he was familiar with the idea that a body in circular motion is subject to a **centrifugal** force. This latter concept was first proposed by the Dutch scientist Christiaan Huygens (1629–1695)—although it is unclear whether Newton got the idea from Huygens or came up with it independently.

If the force of gravity extends from Earth to the moon, maybe it is gravity that holds the moon in its orbit, by counterbalancing the centrifugal force of circular motion. But then, what about the planets? They also move on near-circular orbits, but they go

CHRISTIANUS HUGENIUS
natus 14 Aprilis 1629.
denatus 8 Junii 1695.

Dutch physicist and mathematician Christiaan Huygens was a contemporary of Isaac Newton.

around the sun rather than Earth. Maybe they are held in place by the sun's gravity! Based on this flash of insight, and applying Kepler's third law, Newton worked out that the force of gravity must diminish as the **inverse square** of distance.

At first sight the idea of an "inverse square law" may seem obscure, but it does have precedents. Newton would have been aware that the intensity of light from a candle diminishes as the inverse square of distance, for example. Applying the same idea to gravity, Newton achieved a remarkable result.

> *I compared the force requisite to keep the Moon in her orb with the force of gravity at the surface of the Earth, and found them answer pretty nearly. All this was in the two plague years of 1665–1666. For in those days I was in the prime of my age for invention, and minded mathematics and philosophy more than at any time since.*

These words, written by Newton long after the event, describe one of the greatest moments in the history of science. To show that the force of gravity—the same force we experience ourselves—could also hold the moon in its orbit, was an astonishing breakthrough. It demolished once and for all the old Aristotelian notion of a complete separation between earthly physics and celestial motions. Yet it never seemed to have crossed Newton's mind that perhaps he ought to go public with the discovery.

Why not? Part of the reason may simply have been Newton's personality. He was naturally secretive and seems to have been motivated more by a desire to understand things for himself than to further human knowledge in an altruistic sense. Even years later, when his work on gravity became known to a select group of friends, it required considerable effort to persuade him to write it up and publish it.

There is another possibility. It may be that Newton felt he had not yet answered the most important question at all. Yes, the solar system is held together by the force of gravity. But where does gravity come from?

For Newton, this was the real problem. And it all started with an apple.

Everyone knows that Newton had a sudden flash of insight when he saw an apple fall to the ground in his orchard at Woolsthorpe. Less well known is that what flashed through Newton's mind in that moment was not an answer; it was a question. The question was so simple that no one had ever thought to ask it before.

Why does an apple—or any other dropped object—always fall perpendicularly downward? Regardless of where you are in the orchard, or indeed anywhere on the surface of Earth, the apple always behaves as if the force on it is emanating from the exact center of the planet. Maybe that is literally true, and the source of Earth's gravity is located at its very center. In that case there would have to be other, **analogous** sources at the center of each of the other planets and another at the center of the sun.

Newton realized that it made more sense to assume that every single piece of matter in the universe exerts an attractive force on every other piece. But, if that is so, why is the resultant force straight downward? Why not slightly sideways, toward the atoms in the tree trunk or the farmhouse?

A student today would recognize this as a fairly straightforward problem in integral **calculus**. In layman's terms, that means dividing up all the surrounding matter into infinitesimally small chunks and adding up the force exerted on the apple by each of these chunks.

There is another problem that Newton had glossed over when considering the motion of the moon. Its orbit, like that of the planets, isn't an exact circle: it is an ellipse. When Newton used the formula for centrifugal force to estimate the gravitational force on the moon, he was implicitly assuming a circular orbit. In principle you could tackle the problem of a noncircular orbit using traditional geometric methods, but it would be extremely difficult. A much easier way would be to use calculus again.

Newton could see that, for both these problems, his way forward lay with calculus. He didn't use that word, however, because calculus didn't exist in 1665. Before he could make any further progress, he was going to have to invent it.

4 The Reluctant Scientist

> *I see I have made myself a slave to philosophy.*
>
> Isaac Newton,
> letter to Henry Oldenburg

The threat of plague had abated. In October 1667, soon after he returned to Cambridge, Isaac Newton was elected a fellow of Trinity College. Academic appointments in the seventeenth century were far less onerous than they are today. To all intents and purposes, Newton was free to carry out whatever research work he chose, with only minimal teaching duties. In return, he received board and lodging in the college and a modest stipend of about £60 per year (£9,161 in 2014, about $13,030 US).

F. L. Agate made this replica of the first reflecting telescope, designed by Isaac Newton, which uses a mirror instead of a lens to gather light.

There was just one other thing. All new fellows of the college were required to swear an oath: "I will either set theology as the object of my studies and will take holy orders when the time prescribed by these statutes arrives, or I will resign from the college." In other words, Newton either had to become an ordained priest of the Church of England within the "time prescribed"—seven years—or lose his fellowship.

Faced with the choice between mumbling a few vows or giving up a comfortable job, a more cynical individual might have had no hesitation in jumping at the first option. Not so Newton. He took religion very seriously, and if he was going to endorse the church's doctrine it would only be after he had familiarized himself with every tiny nuance of it. So he started to read all the works of theology he could get his hands on and subjected them to the same kind of painstaking analysis he applied to every other field of study.

Religion wasn't the only new interest Newton acquired around this time. He also became an enthusiastic alchemist. He bought books, a furnace, glassware, and chemicals, and set up a laboratory in a shed adjacent to his college rooms. What the college authorities made of this is not recorded. True alchemy—in the sense of multiplying gold—was still illegal in the 1660s. On the other hand, simply playing with chemicals was a popular hobby among educated gentlemen as long as they were discreet about it. Newton, of course, was the soul of discretion. He was more than happy to keep his alchemical research to himself.

Besides theology and alchemy, Newton's other main activity in the early years of his fellowship was mathematics. More specifically, it was pure mathematics. Despite the progress he had made at Woolsthorpe in the nascent field of applied mathematics—with all his work on gravity and planetary motion—he made no attempt to push these inquiries forward after his return to Cambridge. It doesn't even seem to have crossed his mind to talk about his groundbreaking ideas with anyone. The only research he does seem to have been happy to discuss, in fact, was his work on pure mathematics. This became quite well known, within the confines of the college at least, and Newton soon gained a reputation as something of a mathematical wizard.

One of the first people to recognize Newton's genius was Isaac Barrow. In 1663 he had become Cambridge University's first ever professor of mathematics—a chair endowed by a former MP for the university named Henry Lucas and referred to as the "Lucasian Professorship" in his honor. This has since become one of the most prestigious academic positions in the world—it was held for thirty years by Stephen Hawking, for example. But in those early days it was anything but prestigious, and Barrow was keen to move on to other things. He resigned from the post in 1669, nominating the twenty-seven-year-old Isaac Newton as his successor.

The chair of mathematics was a welcome addition to Newton's college fellowship, bringing in an extra £100 (about US $20,400 in 2014) a year with few extra duties. He was only required to give eight lectures each year, on a subject of his own choosing.

Newton's lectures weren't popular because he talked about subjects that interested him rather than things students needed to know in order to pass their examinations. He was more likely to talk about optical experiments than about binomial expansions. On several occasions he found himself lecturing to an empty room.

Even as a young man, Newton was the archetypal absent-minded professor. According to one of his first biographers, William Stukeley:

> At Cambridge I often heard stories of his absence of mind, from common things of life. As when he has been in the hall at dinner, he has quite neglected to help himself; and the cloth has been taken away before he has eaten anything. [...] That when he had friends to entertain at his chamber, if he stepped into his study for a bottle of wine, and a thought came into his head, he would sit down to paper, and forget his friends.

There is no doubt that Newton was, in modern terms, a workaholic; but "work" meant whatever consumed his curiosity at the time. He was as likely to be engrossed in his theological studies or his alchemical experiments as in the scientific work for which the world remembers him. As his nephew John Conduitt later recalled: "When he was tired with his severer studies of philosophy his only relief and amusement was going to some other study, as history, chronology, divinity and chemistry."

One of the phenomena Newton encountered in the course of his optical experiments was chromatic aberration: a property of lenses that means that different colors come into focus at slightly different distances. As a result, any image formed in this way will appear blurred. This posed a problem for the telescopes of the day, in which light was bent—or refracted, to use the technical term—to a focal point using lenses. Newton took this to mean that an effective refracting telescope—one using lenses—could never be constructed. (He turned out to be wrong on this point, although it was only after his death that a way was found to construct lenses free from chromatic aberration.) Newton's solution was simple and more direct: dispense with lenses altogether and bring light to a focus using a curved mirror instead.

The idea of a reflecting, as opposed to a refracting, telescope had first been proposed in 1663 by the Scottish astronomer James Gregory (1638–1675). But Gregory's telescope never progressed past the drawing board—grinding and polishing a mirror to the required precision was a supreme engineering challenge. It was, however, a challenge that captivated Newton's imagination. All those hours he had spent tinkering with gadgets as a teenager were going to pay off! In 1668 he built the world's first reflecting telescope with his own hands, using tools he also made himself. The resulting instrument was very small—just 9 inches long and 2 inches in diameter (22.86 centimeters by 5.08 cm)—but it proved to be as effective in terms of clarity and magnifying power as a much larger refractor.

Newton showed his telescope to Isaac Barrow, and Barrow showed it to the Royal Society in London. The members instantly fell in love with the new contraption. It represented all the things they held in highest regard: it was an ingenious, meticulously constructed piece of engineering; it worked on recently discovered scientific principles; and it could be used to make astronomical

Isaac Newton revealed that light is made up of colors through his prism experiment in his Woolsthorpe Manor bedroom.

observations beyond the capability of virtually every other telescope of the day.

For the first time, Newton's genius was recognized outside the cloistered confines of Cambridge University. The Royal Society published a brief description of his telescope in 1671, and in January 1672 he was elected a fellow. At around the same time

he wrote down a detailed account of all his optical experiments to date—his work with prisms, light, and color—which served to sweep aside all the old Aristotelian misconceptions about **optics**. His account took the form of a long letter addressed to Henry Oldenburg, the secretary of the Royal Society, but it was soon destined for a much wider audience.

Oldenburg published the letter in its entirety in the February issue of *Philosophical Transactions of the Royal Society*, under the following less than concise heading:

> *A letter of Mr Isaac Newton, Mathematic Professor in the University of Cambridge; containing his new theory about light and colours: where light is declared to be not similar or homogeneal, but consisting of difform rays, some of which are more refrangible than others: and colours are affirmed to be not qualifications of light, derived from refractions of natural bodies (as 'tis generally believed), but original and connate properties, which in divers rays are divers: where several observations and experiments are alleged to prove the said theory.*

Two months after his twenty-ninth birthday, Newton had published his first scientific paper. In terms of its structure, scope, and method, it was arguably the first true scientific paper the world had ever seen.

Robert Hooke was a founding member of the Royal Society and served as its "Curator of Experiments." Hooke and Newton would feud over theories and calculations throughout their careers.

Newton's fame spread. Although the Royal Society had its headquarters in London, its members were located all over Europe. Oldenburg himself had been born in Germany, and his grasp of languages allowed him to build up a sprawling network of correspondents across the Continent and the British Isles. Many of these people were impressed by Newton's discovery—but not all.

Robert Hooke was one of the founding members of the Royal Society. He had started his career as an assistant to Robert Boyle (1627–1691), the grand old man of English science (although he was born in Ireland). Hooke became the Royal Society's "Curator of Experiments," one of the few paid posts in the society. He was an ingenious scientist, bubbling over with ideas—many of them very promising—about every subject under the sun. If he had a weakness it was a lack of mathematical precision, together with an inability to think his ideas through to their logical conclusion.

In many ways, Hooke's personality was the exact opposite of Newton's. The outcome, whenever the two clashed, was a reaction as violent as anything Newton produced in his alchemical laboratory. When Newton published his paper about optics, Hooke was one of the readers who remained unconvinced by it. The result was a long feud between the two men which continued, on and off, until Hooke's death in 1703.

In the four years following the appearance of Newton's paper in *Philosophical Transactions*, the same journal published no fewer than ten letters from Hooke and his allies pointing out supposed flaws in Newton's theory, together with replies from the paper's increasingly exasperated author. The long-running conflict appears to have been encouraged by Oldenburg, who viewed it as good for sales. The fact that Newton always managed to come out on top was to his liking as well—Oldenburg couldn't stand Hooke.

By and large the criticism was not about Newton's experiments exactly. They had been conducted and described with such precision that virtually no one could find fault with them. Instead, the problem lay with Newton's interpretation of his results. Hooke believed these were still consistent with the conventional view, that a prism "adds colour" to a beam of light in an analogous fashion to the way an organ pipe "adds sound" to a flow of air.

The situation foreshadowed many of the later criticisms and misunderstandings Newton was to experience in the course of his career. His primary concern was always to provide an accurate *description* of phenomena; this was true of his work on optics, and it would be true of his later work on gravity. On the other hand, many of his readers—who after all, still thought of themselves as "philosophers" rather than "scientists" (a word that would not exist until the nineteenth century)—were fixated on finding a quasi-metaphysical *interpretation* of phenomena rather than a mere description. To them, it looked as though Newton was trying, and failing, to provide an adequate interpretation of the phenomena he described.

Newton's habitual response to criticism was childlike petulance. He seems to have taken the view that if people failed to appreciate his work, he might as well give up doing that kind of thing altogether. He had better things to do with his time than waste it answering criticisms from the likes of Robert Hooke.

Newton's first threat to resign from the Royal Society came in June 1673, a mere fifteen months after he was elected. And he threatened to do more than simply resign: he was going to abandon natural philosophy altogether. As he wrote to Oldenburg: "I intend to be no further solicitous of matters of philosophy. And therefore I hope you will not take it ill if you find me ever refusing doing anything more in that kind."

Newton did not carry out his threat, although he continued to vent his frustration in letters to Oldenburg. In 1676 he wrote, "I see I have made myself a slave to philosophy," adding, "I will resolutely bid adieu to it eternally, excepting what I do for my private satisfaction, or leave to come out after me; for I see a man must either resolve to put out nothing new, or become a slave to defend it."

This last extract gives an interesting insight into Newton's rather strange way of thinking. It is clear that he objected not to *doing* "philosophy"—or science, as we would say today—but to making the results of his research public. As soon as he did that, he would find himself at the mercy of critics and forced to waste his time answering them. For some reason, the prospect horrified him. He seems, by contrast, to have been perfectly happy with the idea of carrying out research and keeping the results to himself—at least until after he was safely dead!

This time Newton really did carry out his threat—for a few years, at least. He abandoned natural philosophy in favor of other activities that weren't going to attract what he perceived as small-minded and ignorant criticism. He threw yet more effort into

Gottfried Leibniz also claimed to have invented calculus single-handedly.

his private alchemical experiments. These were only ever meant for his personal satisfaction and never intended for publication. Another subject he returned to with renewed enthusiasm was mathematics. He was, after all, Cambridge University's one and only professor of mathematics.

Newton had first hit on the need for some form of "calculus of infinitesimals" at Woolsthorpe in the years 1666–1667. He referred to his version of calculus as the "method of **fluxions**" and seems to have worked it out some time during the 1670s. The date is important because in Germany, Gottfried Leibniz (1646–1716) was working on his own version of calculus at around the same time. A dispute between the two over priority was to dominate their later years.

Both Newton and Leibniz claimed to have invented calculus single-handedly, so the issue at stake was not just who had come up with the idea first, but whether one of them had plagiarized the work of the other. Newton, in particular, believed that Leibniz had stolen the basic ideas of calculus from him. Newton's attitude toward Leibniz wasn't something that developed slowly, over the course of many years: it was there from the very start. His first encounter with the German mathematician came in May 1676, in the form of a letter delivered via Oldenburg acting as an intermediary. Leibniz asked for Newton's advice on the mathematical problem of infinite series, which is related in a roundabout way to calculus. Newton replied in a long letter, again addressed to Oldenburg, who duly passed it on.

The process was repeated again that October: a letter from Leibniz to Newton via Oldenburg, followed by a reply from Newton to Leibniz, once again through Oldenburg. But this time Newton must have felt that Leibniz was getting uncomfortably close to his method of fluxions, which at this stage he wanted to keep to himself. So when he got to a critical step in his reply to Leibniz, he wrote it down in the form of a cryptogram—a code that was completely undecipherable without the cryptographic key! Newton carefully kept the key in his files and produced it many years later when he was attempting to prove his priority in the calculus dispute.

Of course, the fact that Leibniz received an impenetrable coded message from Newton—even if it did hint at the latter's method of fluxions—does not prove that Leibniz was guilty of plagiarism. What it does prove, however, is that Newton was deeply suspicious and untrusting—almost to the point of paranoia.

When Henry Oldenburg died in 1677, the Royal Society appointed a new secretary. That person, to Newton's dismay, was Robert Hooke. Two years later, Newton received some unwelcome correspondence from him. It was unwelcome not because it was critical of Newton's work—on this occasion Hooke went out of his way to be polite—but because it related to natural philosophy, which Newton was genuinely trying to avoid at the time. In his letter, Hooke made the suggestion that the moon's near-circular orbit around Earth was the result of two separate and mutually conflicting effects. First, there was a tendency to

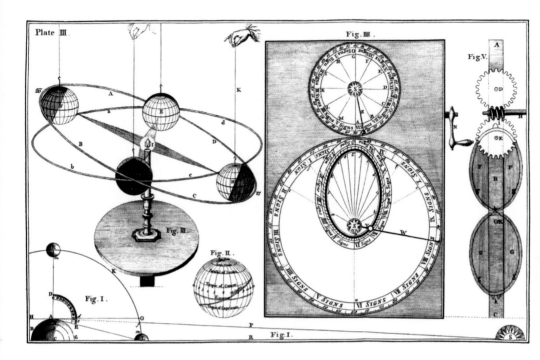

James Ferguson's ecliptic diagram, published in 1756, illustrated Isaac Newton's principles. In Figure I, the moon orbits around Earth (*bottom left*), and in Figure III (*left*), the seasons are explained by Earth's axis as it orbits the sun.

move in a straight line tangential to the orbit, and then there was a downward force—essentially at right angles to the first motion—due to the gravitational attraction of Earth.

In layman's terms, this is a pretty good summary of the way scientists now understand the moon's motion in terms of Newton's theory of gravity. Surprisingly, however, Newton replied to Hooke that he had never heard of this hypothesis before. Even by this date, it seems, Newton had not fully worked out all the implications of his earlier musings on the subject of gravity and the moon. Hooke was rapidly catching up—he also mentioned the inverse square law in his letter, for example—and possibly even in danger of overtaking him.

To put Hooke in his place, Newton decided to consider a more sophisticated gravitational problem than that of the moon's orbit. In his reply to Hooke's letter, he attempted to sketch the path a body would follow if it were dropped toward a **point mass** with only a very small tangential velocity, far less than that required for a circular orbit.

For whatever reason, the diagram Newton drew was wrong. He showed the object spiraling in toward the center. The correct answer is a highly elongated ellipse, with the point mass at one focus. Simply based on Kepler's laws, Newton should have understood this. Maybe he did understand it and was working in a furious red haze because he always got that way when he was writing to Hooke.

Hooke may not have been a mathematical genius, but even he could see at a glance that Newton had made a mistake. He replied with his own diagram, which was at least qualitatively correct in that it depicted an elliptical orbit. But he made the error of putting the point mass at the center of the ellipse rather than at one focus. It was only after Newton saw Hooke's not-quite-right ellipse that he finally drew the correct form of orbit.

The argument continued to simmer in Hooke's mind. A few years later, it would flare up again, only this time it would threaten to ruin Newton's finest hour.

PHILOSOPHIÆ

NATURALIS

PRINCIPIA

MATHEMATICA.

Autore *IS. NEWTON*, *Trin. Coll. Cantab. Soc.* Matheseos
Professore *Lucasiano*, & Societatis Regalis Sodali.

IMPRIMATUR·

S. PEPYS, *Reg. Soc.* PRÆSES.

Julii 5. 1686.

LONDINI,

Jussu *Societatis Regiæ* ac Typis *Josephi Streater*. Prostat apud
plures Bibliopolas. *Anno* MDCLXXXVII.

Applied Mathematics

... to discover the forces of nature from the phenomena of motions ...

**Isaac Newton,
from The Principia**

Early in 1684, three men were having an animated discussion in one of London's fashionable coffeehouses. The oldest of the trio was the most famous: Sir Christopher Wren (1632–1723), the man who had designed St. Paul's Cathedral and many other fine churches in the city. Although he had made his name as an architect, Wren's earliest work had been in the field of astronomy—a subject in which he retained a keen interest.

This is the title page from the first edition of Isaac Newton's *Philosophiae Naturalis Principia Mathematica.*

It was an astronomical problem the three men were discussing in the coffeehouse that day.

Also present was Robert Hooke—not as famous as Wren, but at forty-nine only three years younger. The third man, by contrast, was a mere youngster of twenty-eight. His name was Edmond Halley (1656–1742), and he was already making a name for himself as one of the country's leading observational astronomers. Like Hooke and Wren, Halley was a fellow of the Royal Society.

The three men were arguing about planetary orbits. Each of them, it seems, had independently come to the conclusion that the force holding a planet in its orbit varied as the inverse square of distance. This followed from two mathematical relationships that were well established by that time—Kepler's third law and Huygens's formula for centrifugal force. Newton, of course, had accepted this line of logic as long ago as 1666, during his enforced vacation at Woolsthorpe.

The three men agreed about something else as well. They knew that the resulting orbit was an ellipse, according to Kepler's first law. But was there a cause-and-effect relationship between these two facts? Did an inverse square law necessarily imply an elliptical orbit?

Hooke maintained that it did and that he could prove the point mathematically. The other two were skeptical: they knew from experience that Hooke was far from being a mathematical genius. To call his bluff, Wren offered him a prize worth 40 shillings

English astronomer Edmund Halley observed the comet that would be named for him in 1682. Halley calculated the comet's orbit and predicted its return in 1758.

(about $400 US in 2014) if he could provide a mathematical proof within two months. To no one's surprise, the deadline came and went without a response.

But the problem didn't go away. Young Halley, for one, couldn't stop thinking about it. What shape of orbit results from an inverse square law of force? It was a simple enough question, and he wanted an answer to it.

Halley was acquainted with the brilliant, if slightly eccentric, professor of mathematics at Cambridge University. Maybe he would be able to help? Halley made the journey to Trinity College in August 1684 and paid a visit to Newton. After explaining the background, he took a deep breath and asked him the big question: How would a planet move if it were subject to a force that varied as the inverse square of distance?

Without hesitation, Newton answered that the planet would follow an elliptical orbit. When Halley asked him how he could be so sure, he was astonished to hear Newton's reply: "Why, I have calculated it." Unfortunately, even after much frantic searching, Newton couldn't lay his hands on the proof he was sure he had written down somewhere. He promised Halley that he would redo the calculations and send them on to him later.

Newton was as good as his word. In November 1684 he sent Halley a nine-page manuscript written in Latin, entitled "*De Motu Corporum in Gyrum*" ("On the Motion of Bodies in Orbit"). Despite its brevity, the manuscript did more than simply answer Halley's original question. Using standard geometrical methods, Newton succeeded in deriving all three of Kepler's laws of planetary motion, starting from a few basic assumptions about the forces involved.

Halley was impressed. He wrote to Newton asking him to put a final polish on the manuscript so that it could be published by the Royal Society. That, Halley assumed, would be the work of a few weeks at most. He was wrong. As it turned out, he had to wait more than a year before he saw the revised manuscript. It was worth the wait. By the time Newton had finished, his nine-page manuscript had grown into the greatest scientific treatise the world had ever seen.

Newton hadn't planned it that way. He was still irritated by the whole subject of "natural philosophy," viewing it as something he had found interesting in the past but from which he had long since moved on. He would have been happy to get Halley's manuscript out of the way as quickly as possible. But as he started to work on it, he saw vistas of previously undreamed-of possibility opening up before him. The same line of thinking he had used to connect mathematics to planetary motion could be applied to other things as well—possibly even to *everything*. The manuscript started to grow—and so did Newton's enthusiasm.

He began to perceive that "the whole difficulty of philosophy seems to be to discover the forces of nature from the phenomena of motions and then to demonstrate the other phenomena from these forces." Sir Francis Bacon had said much the same thing sixty years earlier but Newton made a crucial extra step. He recognized that this entire cycle of discovery and demonstration could be achieved through the medium of mathematics. It was the great breakthrough the scientific world had been waiting for.

It took Newton eighteen months to write the book he called *Philosophiae Naturalis Principia Mathematica*—"Mathematical Principles of Natural Philosophy." The very title points to an astonishing revolution in world view. In the seventeenth century, mathematics was seen as elegant, ordered, and predictable. Natural philosophy—the study of the physical world—was none of those things. Or at least not until Isaac Newton got hold of it.

It is virtually certain that Newton derived all the main results of the *Principia* using his "secret" method of fluxions—calculus, in other words. But he wanted to keep that technique to himself, so he laboriously translated all the proofs into traditional geometric form for publication. He gave the *Principia* the standard format of an ancient mathematical treatise, complete with theorems, propositions, proofs, and corollaries. Coupled with the fact that it was written in Latin, the book's turgid style would have looked old-fashioned and abstruse even in Newton's time.

This was no accident. If the *Principia* was difficult to read, it was because that is how the author planned it. Newton was still pathologically averse to criticism of any kind. He was convinced the only reason anyone could have for faulting his work was that they were too ignorant to understand it. So what could he do to minimize the number of ignorant people who would read the book? Making it as obscure as possible would certainly help him "to avoid being baited by little smatterers in mathematics," as he explained later.

The *Principia* is organized in three sections, which Newton called "books" even though it was published as a single volume. The first book is a greatly expanded version of the earlier manuscript he sent to Halley, "*De Motu Corporum in Gyrum.*" Book 2 deals with the motion of bodies when they are immersed in a surrounding

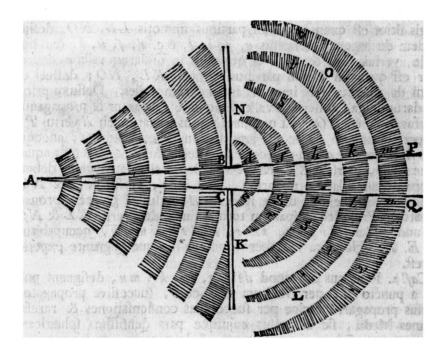

The calculations in Newton's *Principia* were explained through complex geometric forms because he wanted to keep his method of fluxions secret.

medium rather than a vacuum—including, *inter alia*, a detailed mathematical refutation of Descartes's **theory of vortices**. It is the third book that finally reveals the true scope and power of the Newtonian approach. Called "*De Mundi Systemate*," "On the System of the World," it describes the practical application of the theory developed in the first two books to the motion of the moon, the planets, the satellites of Jupiter, several recently observed comets, and even the previously baffling phenomenon of Earth's tides.

The genius of the *Principia* lies in the way Newton applies rigorous mathematical methods to the previously intractable problems of the physical world. He follows a logical train of thought all the way from first principles through to observable phenomena. Even here, he was standing on the shoulders of giants. For the most part, the "first principles" he drew on had already been propounded by others. Concepts such as inertia and momentum would have been familiar to Galileo half a century earlier.

At the outset of Book 1, Newton lays out his three laws of motion:

> *Law 1: Every body perseveres in its state of rest, or of uniform motion in a right line, unless it is compelled to change that state by forces impressed thereon.*

> *Law 2: The alteration of motion is ever proportional to the motive force impressed; and*

is made in the direction of the right line in which that force is impressed.

Law 3: To every action there is always opposed an equal reaction: or the mutual actions of two bodies upon each other are always equal, and directed to contrary parts.

Perhaps the most significant feature of these three laws is that each of them flies in the face of Aristotelian "common sense." Aristotle stated that moving objects tend to slow down unless you apply a force to keep them going—which seems to accord with our everyday experience. But here was Newton claiming the very opposite: that an object will continue to move *unless* you apply a force to slow it down.

Even today, many science-fiction movies can be counted on to break all three of Newton's laws at some point during the special effects sequences. There is a good reason for this. If the special effects people strictly obeyed Newton's laws, most members of the audience would think they had made a mistake. That's how counterintuitive the first three statements in the *Principia* are!

The other big idea Newton introduced in the *Principia* was his famous "law of gravity": every particle in the universe attracts every other particle with a force that is proportional to the product of their masses and inversely proportional to the square of the distance between them. Using calculus—carefully disguised as classical geometry—he demonstrated that a spherical body such as the sun or a planet will exert exactly the same gravitational attraction as a single point, of the same mass, located at its center.

What made Newton's work different from anything that had gone before was its predictive power. His talk about forces and orbits was precision mathematics. He did not have to limit himself to approximating planetary orbits as circles or planetary bodies as perfect spheres. He could treat elliptical orbits and non-spherical bodies with exactly the same mathematical apparatus.

And he could go further still. For the first time in history, he found a convincing way to explain the tiny perturbations astronomers had observed in the motion of the moon. An ellipse is the orbit you get if you focus solely on the moon going around Earth, in isolation from the rest of the universe. In reality, the situation is more complicated than that. At the very least, you have to consider the three-body system of Earth, moon, and sun. When Newton did so, he found that the moon's orbit turned into a perturbed ellipse very much like the one that is actually observed.

Book 1 of the *Principia* was finished by April 1686, and Newton duly sent the manuscript off to the Royal Society. Its president at the time was none other than Samuel Pepys (1633–1703), a man best known today for his posthumously published diary. In his lifetime, however, Pepys had a reputation as a competent administrator, and it was on this basis—rather than any great scientific achievement—that he had secured the presidency of the Royal Society. In this capacity, Pepys agreed to provide the imprimatur for the publication of the *Principia* on one condition:

Samuel Pepys, 1666, was president of the Royal Society and was involved in the publication of *Principia*.

someone else was going to have to pay for it. The society was short of cash and was not prepared to risk as much as a penny toward the cost of publishing so abstruse a book.

That might have been the end of the *Principia*, if the man who proposed it in the first place, Edmond Halley, had not come to the rescue. He offered to bear all the costs of publication himself and even undertook to edit the entire text single-handed.

As far as Newton was concerned, things were looking up. Little did he suspect that a long-forgotten argument was about to resurface.

It was only to be expected that Hooke, as an officer of the Royal Society, would find out sooner or later that his long-time rival was about to publish a new book about planetary motions. Hooke automatically assumed the book had grown out of his own earlier discussions with Newton. That was not an unreasonable assumption; there may even have been some truth to it.

It was equally reasonable, under the circumstances, that Hooke should feel Newton owed him an acknowledgement for his role in the process. But what was his role, exactly? Hooke had one view on the subject; Newton had another. Hooke expressed his view in a letter to Halley, and the latter duly passed it on to Newton: "Mr Hooke has some pretensions upon the invention of the rule of the decrease of gravity. He says you had the notion from him and seems to expect you should make some mention of him in the preface."

Newton was appalled by the suggestion. He felt that Hooke's contribution had been trivial and that he had done all the hard work himself. He complained to Halley that if Hooke had his way, "Mathematicians that find out, settle and do all the business must content themselves with being nothing but dry calculators and drudges and another that does nothing but pretend and grasp at all things must carry away all the invention."

This reaction is interesting. It gets close to acknowledging that Hooke did indeed come up with a few ideas of his own, but that he just threw them out in scattershot fashion without knowing how to develop or test them. As far as Newton was concerned, if he picked up one of Hooke's discarded ideas and made it work, then the credit should be due to him. It is a contentious point. Arguments of this type often crop up in creative endeavors involving more than one individual. Some people will agree wholeheartedly with Newton; others may feel that Hooke had a point.

One thing was beyond dispute, however, Newton was never going to submit to what he regarded as intellectual blackmail. He was so annoyed he threatened to stop work then and there, before he had completed the third book. He wrote to Halley: "Philosophy is such an impertinently litigious lady, that a man had as good be engaged in lawsuits, as have to do with her. I found it so formerly, and now I am no sooner come near her again, but she gives me warning."

Fortunately for posterity, Halley eventually managed to calm Newton down. The *Principia* finally saw print in the summer of 1687. Tucked away inside was a brief statement to the effect that the inverse square law had previously been "severally observed" by Hooke, Wren, and Halley.

J. Newton

6 Action and Reaction

Publication of the *Principia* made Newton an instant celebrity. It was widely recognized as a work of genius, albeit a highly obscure one. As in the case of *A Brief History of Time*, written almost exactly three hundred years later by another Lucasian Professor, Stephen Hawking, it became the fashionable thing to own a copy, if not necessarily to read it—let alone try to understand it. According to an oft-quoted anecdote, a student at Cambridge once supposedly remarked, as Newton

Publication of the *Principia*, though contested by some of his peers and difficult to understand, catapulted Isaac Newton to scientific infamy.

passed by, "There goes a man that writ a book that neither he nor anybody else understands."

The *Principia* was given a particularly favorable reception by the scientific community in England, which soon developed what amounted to a patriotic pride in Newton's achievement. The most persistent voice of opposition was silenced when Hooke died in March 1703. Later the same year, Newton was elected president of the Royal Society—and he continued to be re-elected to that post every year for the rest of his life.

On the other side of the channel, praise for the *Principia* was more muted. The general reaction on the Continent fell into two camps. As with the earlier controversy over Newton's optical experiments, there was a split between readers who focused on the descriptive power of Newton's theories—who applauded the work—and those who focused on his failure to provide a convincing interpretation of his results—who were far more critical. The French *Journal des Savants*, for example, claimed the *Principia* was "devoid of physical value, because it did not satisfy the conditions required by the intelligibility of the universe."

Among the book's most vocal opponents were the followers of Descartes, the French philosopher who had championed a mechanistic view of the universe half a century before the *Principia* was written. Their main objection was to the apparently "occult" notion of action at a distance. In Newton's theory, gravity was an invisible force that extended indefinitely through empty space. To many people, this looked like a step backward from

Descartes's theory of vortices to the superstition and mysticism of the Middle Ages.

Another point of contention was Newton's use of the word "attraction" to describe gravitational force. "Attraction" is a perfectly acceptable scientific term these days, but to Newton's original readers the word implied some kind of conscious "liking," analogous to the way one human being may be attracted to another. Leibniz, Newton's great rival in the development of calculus, described the Newtonian concept of attraction as "a return to occult quantities and, even worse, to inexplicable ones." By "return" he may have been alluding to the magical concepts of "sympathy" and "attraction" as expounded in the medieval **Hermetica**, or esoteric wisdom texts.

For his part, Newton believed that gravitational attraction would turn out to have a perfectly rational explanation—even though he freely admitted he had no idea what that explanation might be:

> *These principles I consider not as occult qualities, supposed to result from the specific forms of things, but as general laws of Nature, by which the things themselves are formed: their truth appearing to us by phenomena, though their causes be not yet discovered.*

This quotation comes from Newton's second major work, *Opticks*, the first version of which was presented to the Royal Society in 1704, a few months after his election as its president. Unlike the

Principia, the new book was written in English and contained very little in the way of mathematics, making it much easier to read.

As the title suggests, the book is largely devoted to Newton's work on optics—the study of light and color that he had embarked on at Woolsthorpe in 1666. Large parts of the book had been written long before it finally saw print. Some sections, in fact, are almost verbatim transcripts of the optical lectures he had given as a young professor more than thirty years earlier.

As with the *Principia*, the publication of *Opticks* stirred up controversy. There were two areas of contention. The first was over the nature of color. Old-timers still believed, like Aristotle, that white light was pure and colorless and that color was added to it as it passed through material objects. According to Newton, his experiments with prisms proved that this was not the case. Instead, he argued that all the colors of the spectrum were already present in white light and simply separated out when they interacted with matter.

The second controversy concerned the nature of light. The Dutch scientist Huygens had proposed a wave theory, by analogy with the behavior of waves in water. Newton favored what he called the corpuscular theory—the idea that light was made up of a stream of minutely small particles.

It is no coincidence that *Opticks* was published less than a year after Hooke's death. Hooke had opposed Newton on both points. He believed white light to be intrinsically colorless, and he believed it propagated in a wave-like rather than a particle-

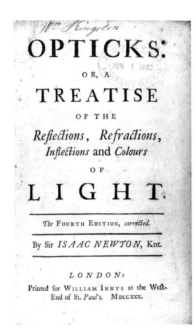

Isaac Newton finally published his theories on light in *Opticks* after the death of Robert Hooke, one of his major opponents.

like way. Newton knew only too well that if he published the book before Hooke's death, he would find himself embroiled in endless argument. So, as he openly admitted in the preface to the published version, "To avoid being engaged in disputes about these matters, I have hitherto delayed the printing, and should still have delayed it, had not the importunity of friends prevailed upon me."

As it was, both controversies bubbled on for decades—even the less contentious one about the nature of color. As late as 1810, the great German polymath Johann Wolfgang von Goethe produced a book, *The Theory of Colours*, which was specifically aimed at refuting Newton's theory and restoring the Aristotelian notion of pure white light. By that time, however, few people were prepared to take Goethe's arguments seriously.

Subsequent discoveries proved beyond doubt that Newton was right and that white light is indeed made up of different colors. Ironically, the final proof of this is intimately tied to the wave theory of light—a theory Newton himself had dismissed. We now know that each color corresponds to a specific wavelength of light and that light containing many different wavelengths appears white.

In the modern world of **quantum theory**, the accepted view is that light has a dual nature. Under some conditions it behaves like a wave and in other circumstances like a particle. Does this mean that Newton and Hooke were both right? Charitably, we might say that it does—although it is probably more accurate to come down on the side of Hooke in this instance. By and large the conditions under which light behaves like a particle were unknown in Newton's time. All the experiments he carried out himself are more easily explained in terms of waves than particles.

Opticks ends with a series of "queries." In the first edition of 1704, there were sixteen of these. When the book was translated into Latin in 1706, the number of queries had risen to twenty-three. It continued to rise with each subsequent printing. By the time the fourth and final edition was published, posthumously in 1730, the book contained no fewer than thirty-one.

Although Newton called them "queries," they are actually speculations. He framed them in the form of a question, rather than a statement, because they were things he could not prove— even though he believed them to be true. The wording is often tortuous, but Newton's meaning comes through clearly enough. The very first query, for example, reads: "Do not bodies act upon light at a distance, and by their action bend its rays; and is not this action strongest at the least distance?"

As the queries progress, they stray from optics onto other unrelated subjects: heat, magnetism, static electricity, gravity, the composition of matter, chemical reactions. At the same time, the queries get steadily longer. The last of them, Query 31, stretches for over thirty pages! While Newton's speculations have not always stood the test of time, they pointed the way toward some of the key problems that would dominate physical science for the next two hundred years. This was exactly what Newton intended. "I have only begun the analysis of what remains to be discovered," he wrote, "hinting several things about it, and leaving the hints to be examined and improved by the farther experiments and observations of such as are inquisitive."

Opticks wasn't the only book Newton added to over the years. When the second Latin edition of the *Principia* was published in 1713, he appended a new section at the end called "*Scholium Generale*," usually rendered in English as "General Scholium." His main aim here was to underline the superiority of his quantitative approach over the qualitative approach of Descartes. Newton considered the latter to be founded on vague "hypotheses"—a word he almost always used as if it were a pejorative. The General Scholium is notable for containing the *Principia*'s only well-known quotation: *hypotheses non fingo*—"I do not contrive hypotheses."

In modern scientific jargon, the word "hypothesis" refers to any testable assumption—not a particularly distasteful thing in itself. But to Newton, "hypothesis" seems to have signified "unsupported interpretation of the facts." In that sense, it is quite true that Newton does not contrive any hypotheses in the *Principia*. He does in *Opticks*, however, which contains the subsequently disproved "hypothesis" that light propagates like a stream of particles. Significantly, that was one of the few times Newton slipped up in his scientific work.

There are no such oversights in the *Principia*. Newton did not venture a single statement he could not justify with rigorous mathematics. As he asserted in the General Scholium: "To us it is enough that gravity does really exist, and act according to the laws which we have explained." Privately, however, Newton did not believe in gravity's "action at a distance" any more than the followers of Descartes did. In a letter to a fellow academic in 1693, he expressed his opinion: "It is inconceivable that inanimate brute matter should, without the mediation of something else which is not material, operate upon and affect other matter without mutual contact."

In the course of revising the *Principia*, Newton made a new enemy—probably the second greatest bane of his life after Hooke.

This was John Flamsteed (1646–1719), who had become England's first Astronomer Royal in 1675. One of the things Newton hoped to do in the new version of the book was to increase the accuracy of his predictions concerning the moon's orbit. But he could only do that with the aid of the latest observations—and Flamsteed was sitting on them.

In some ways, Newton's confrontation with Flamsteed was the mirror image of his earlier conflict with Hooke. When Hooke had been puzzling over the problem of orbits, he had found himself in desperate need of something Newton could supply—his mathematical expertise—while Newton, for his part, was driven by an almost paranoid desire to keep his mathematical secrets to himself. Now the tables were turned. It was Flamsteed who had something Newton wanted—his observational data—and it was the Astronomer Royal who was displaying an obsession with secrecy.

In the end Newton, with the assistance of Halley, tricked Flamsteed into handing over his observations by telling him that Prince George of Denmark, the husband of Queen Anne, wished to have them published. In fact, Newton and Halley published an unauthorized, incomplete copy of Flamsteed's work, leaving the latter bitter and humiliated. The Astronomer Royal was forced to buy up as many copies as he could and burn them. This is one of the few episodes in Newton's life that even his most enthusiastic biographers have trouble putting a positive spin on.

Isaac Newton needed the astronomical observations of John Flamsteed and made an enemy of the astronomer by tricking Flamsteed into releasing them.

At least Newton dealt with Flamsteed face-to-face. His other bête noire in the post-Hooke years was based overseas. In 1684, the German mathematician Leibniz published details of a powerful new mathematical technique that he referred to as calculus. It was virtually identical to the "method of fluxions" Newton had been using for years. Unfortunately for Newton, but inevitable in light of his habitual secrecy, almost no one was aware of his method. He did not publish a full account of it until

1704, when he appended a short Latin treatise on the subject to the first edition of *Opticks*.

The bitter "priority dispute" over the invention of calculus ran on for years, even after the death of Leibniz in 1716. Who worked it out first? Did Newton steal the idea from Leibniz, or did Leibniz steal it from Newton? Few observers seemed prepared to accept the obvious answer: that the two men—both mathematical geniuses— had developed their techniques separately and independently of each other. They adopted different technical terms and different notation, and they used the results in completely different ways for different purposes. Leibniz was a pure mathematician who was only interested in abstract problems, whereas Newton was looking for a form of mathematics that could be applied to the mechanics of motion.

The calculus dispute became a matter of national pride, as English-speaking intellectuals sided with Newton and their German-speaking counterparts aligned themselves with Leibniz. It was an echo of the earlier "English versus French pride" conflict between Newton's supporters and those of Descartes, which had flared up in the wake of the *Principia*.

In 1712, in what might be considered a rather naive move, Leibniz appealed to that quintessentially English institution, the Royal Society, to arbitrate in the controversy. Newton, who just happened to be the society's president at the time, duly appointed a committee to investigate. Not surprisingly, perhaps, the committee concluded in Newton's favor.

From Physics to Metaphysics

7

> *Newton was not the first of the age of reason. He was the last of the magicians.*
>
> Maynard Keynes,
> "Newton, the Man"

Religion played a much bigger part in life in the seventeenth century than it does today. For much of the period Europe was riven with conflict between one version of Christianity and another. When Newton was born in 1642, England was being torn apart by a civil war. At its heart was a clash between rival Protestant factions, the established Church of England and the reformist Puritans. By the time Newton reached adulthood, the crown and the Church of England had

An artistic rendering of an alchemist in his laboratory

been restored to power, but it was the Puritans who dominated public life during the influential decade he spent at school.

English middle-class society—and middle-class intellectual life in particular—revolved around the clergy. When Newton's mother left home to remarry, consigning her three-year-old son to the care of his grandparents, her new husband was the rector of a neighboring village, regarded as a pretty good catch. Her own brother was also a clergyman: the Reverend William Ayscough (it was he who encouraged Newton to apply for a place at Trinity College). And when Newton became a fellow of Trinity in 1667, it was on condition that he, too, would take holy orders within seven years.

Prior to this point, there is no evidence that Newton had taken any particular interest in religious matters. It is clear from his early writings that he was a firm believer in God, but such a belief was virtually universal at the time. When the young Newton read, it was about science and philosophy, not theology. All that changed when he was awarded the college fellowship. Newton now had an obligation, as he saw it, to learn everything he could about the Christian religion. After all, how could he be expected to take vows on a subject he was less than completely familiar with?

The result was an unexpected crisis. The more Newton read, the more certain he became that the Church of England was wrong on certain fundamental matters of doctrine. One tenet in particular Newton found himself unable to accept. Ironically—because his association with Trinity College was the reason for his interest in the subject—the doctrine that gave him such trouble was the concept of the Holy Trinity. As far as Newton could see, there was nothing to support this view in the Bible, which he regarded as the ultimate authority on all religious matters. To his mind, that could mean only one thing: the doctrine of the Trinity was wrong.

When Newton accepted his fellowship in 1667, he swore that he would either take Holy Orders within seven years or resign from the college. As the deadline approached, he quietly prepared to resign. He saw no alternative. He would like to have continued with his work at Cambridge, but he was not prepared to take an oath he believed to be false.

At the last minute, he spotted a loophole that offered a glimmer of hope. In addition to his fellowship, he held another post at Cambridge as Lucasian Professor of Mathematics. This was a recently created position and, unlike older professorships, it carried no explicit religious duties. Newton proposed, therefore, that the Lucasian Professor should be excused from any requirements to take Holy Orders. With the support of the previous holder of the post, Isaac Barrow, the proposition was put to no less an authority than the king himself, Charles II. A royal mandate was duly issued releasing the Lucasian professorship, in perpetuity, from any religious obligation. Newton was free to pursue his academic work for as long as he wished.

When Charles II died in 1685, the crown passed to his younger brother, James II, a Roman Catholic. In 1687 he attempted to introduce Catholic scholars to Cambridge University on an equal footing with Protestants. Not everyone approved such religious tolerance, however. Newton was one of the eminent figures who vigorously defended the university's exclusively Protestant status against the wishes of the Catholic monarch.

The following year saw the Glorious Revolution—and the overthrow of James II, who fled to the Continent. The Protestant

After the Glorious Revolution that deposed James II, William of Orange arrives in England on November 5, 1688, and becomes king of Great Britain and Ireland on April 11, 1689.

William of Orange was invited to assume the British throne in his place. The so-called Convention Parliament of 1689, which formalized this arrangement, contained within it two members from Cambridge University, one of whom was none other than Professor Isaac Newton—his reward for standing up against King James. There is no record of Newton doing anything in Parliament other than voting in favor of William III. He went on to serve a second brief term as a member of Parliament in 1701–1702, although this, too, proved to be uneventful.

Even though the threat of ordination no longer hung over him after 1674, Newton's interest in theology showed no sign of diminishing. He remained fascinated by the subject for the rest of his life and felt he was just as likely to gain an insight into the true nature of reality from a religious text as from any scientific experiment. His personal library contained more than thirty versions of the Bible in various languages—including the original Hebrew, which he taught himself to read. He also possessed dozens of theological texts, from the early church fathers to ecclesiastical authors of his own time. For his own part, he produced an estimated million and a half words of biblical analysis, much of it never published, on subjects ranging from ancient chronology to the ending of the world.

For as long as Christianity has existed, people have been offering "predictions" of the date of the apocalypse based on their own particular interpretation of the Bible. In most cases, the predicted date is only a few years, or even months, away from the time the prophecy is announced. This annoyed Newton inordinately. Every time such a prediction failed to be fulfilled, it made the Bible look ridiculous and tended to diminish what he saw as its supreme authority. So he made a careful prediction of his own, which safely placed the end of the world (or, more accurately, the Second Coming of Christ) in the far distant future.

Newton's conclusion was that the mysterious "time, times and half-time" referred to in the Bible would "not end before 2060." That date now seems far more imminent. As early as 2003, the front page of the *Daily Telegraph* was carrying the scaremongering—if not entirely accurate—headline "Newton Set 2060 for End of World."

The more he read, the more Newton became convinced that both Protestant and Catholic churches had gone astray. In his view, only the most ancient scriptures, in their original untranslated form, were capable of revealing "the true religion of the sons of Noah before it began to be corrupted by the worship of false gods."

Although Newton had arrived at these unorthodox religious views on his own, he discovered they were not unique to him. In 1690 he began a correspondence with the philosopher John Locke (1632–1704), who had independently come to similar conclusions. Like Newton, Locke was recognized as one of the towering figures of the English intellectual world. Thomas Jefferson, for example, wrote that he considered Francis Bacon, John Locke, and Isaac Newton to be "the three greatest men that have ever lived, without any exception."

Isaac Newton corresponded with British philosopher John Locke. The two shared viewpoints on religious matters, concerning the Holy Trinity and the divinity of Christ.

Locke was as unconvinced by the doctrine of the Trinity as Newton. Both men believed it to be a post-biblical invention and that the divinity of Christ was not mentioned anywhere in the earliest versions of the New Testament. Newton expounded this view in an extensive treatise entitled "An Historical Account of Two Notable Corruptions of Scripture," which he sent privately to Locke in November 1690. The book was eventually published in 1754, long after they were both dead.

It was during the 1690s that Newton's other "metaphysical" interest—alchemy—reached its dramatic climax. The subject had fascinated him for years; his interest may have been sparked as a teenager, when he was lodging in the house of an apothecary. Within months of settling down to life as a fellow of Trinity, he had made a fully equipped alchemical laboratory in a shed that abutted his rooms. There he happily carried out experiments, night and day, whenever he had the chance—even while he was busy writing the *Principia*.

Newton wasn't just a dabbler in alchemy; he was following a careful and methodical program. He read everything he could. A third of his library, 169 books, was devoted to the topic. He made meticulous notes—more than a million words—recording his experiments and his speculations. Much of this was written in a private code that has yet to be deciphered.

In his alchemical writings, Newton adopted a pseudonym—an anagram of the Latin version of his name, Isaacus Neuutonus. It was an anagram with grandiose pretensions: *Jeova Sanctus*

Unus (in Latin, the letters J and I are interchangeable, as are U and V). This is often interpreted to mean "the one true God"—not perhaps a literal translation, but certainly a clear statement of Newton's anti-Trinitarian beliefs.

Some modern-day apologists have claimed that Newton wasn't really an alchemist at all, but a pioneer of chemistry. But there was a clear and recognized difference between the two disciplines, even in Newton's time. Alchemy was focused on the transmutation of metals and was rooted in traditions handed down since ancient times, often with a distinctly mystical flavor. Chemistry, on the other hand, was the study of chemical interactions using the new scientific method. It is certainly true that Newton adopted a more rigorous approach than any alchemist before him—weighing, measuring, timing, and recording reactions with meticulous precision. But it is clear from his writings that his goal was identical to that of any other alchemist, namely the discovery of the Philosopher's Stone. This was the legendary key to the secret of "multiplying gold"—the ability to combine a small seed of gold with other, lesser, metals and turn the whole mixture into pure gold.

John Maynard Keynes once made a striking observation: "Newton was not the first of the age of reason. He was the last of the magicians." Unpalatable as it may seem to some people, Newton's world view was not that of a modern scientist; it was that of an alchemist. He believed in the reality of both the material and spiritual worlds and that all material things had a spiritual counterpart. He believed in the power of signs and symbols, and he believed there was a single great secret connecting heaven to earth, matter to spirit. When he witnessed chemical reactions and transformations in his laboratory, he saw them as a magical manifestation of this great, cosmic secret.

One of the variables Newton wanted to record in his laboratory was temperature. To this end he devised his own form of thermometer and his own scale of temperature. As in the modern Celsius system, he defined the freezing point of water as zero degrees. But, rather than assigning an obvious figure like 100 degrees to boiling point, he referred to it as the "33rd degree." Why 33? No one really knows, although some people—including the historically-not-always-accurate novelist Dan Brown—have suggested Newton was influenced by the traditional mystical associations of the number 33.

Alchemists were habitually secretive about their work, frequently using ciphers and anagrams in their writings. This suited Newton's personality perfectly. There were two very good reasons for such secrecy. The first was that alchemical knowledge was considered, as Newton himself put it, "not to be communicated without immense danger to the world." The second reason for remaining discreet was that alchemists were viewed with suspicion by the authorities, chiefly due to the prevalence among them of frauds and charlatans.

Indeed, claiming to be able to "multiply gold," or making any attempt to do so, was illegal in England until 1689. It was only in that year that the Act against Multipliers was repealed, after successful lobbying by the aging pioneer of the Royal Society, Robert Boyle. Boyle was widely considered to be one of the most successful alchemists of the day. He was among the few people Newton looked up to. Newton suspected that Boyle might even have succeeded in the quest to multiply gold. Needless to say, he was keen to catch up. When Boyle died in 1691, Newton—with a somewhat bewildered Locke acting as intermediary—managed to get hold of some of the older man's notes and materials. He set to work, more eagerly than ever, to see what he could make of them.

Newton's most important alchemical work, finished in 1693, was a long paper entitled "Praxis." Like all his writings on the subject, it was strictly private and never intended for publication. At the very end of the manuscript he appears to claim to have had success in multiplying gold:

> *You may multiply it in quantity by the mercuries of which you made it at first, amalgaming the stone with the mercury of three or more eagles and adding their weight of the water, and if you design it for metals you may melt every time three parts of gold with one of the stone. Every multiplication will increase its virtue ten times and, if you use the mercury of the second and third rotation without the spirit, perhaps a thousand times. Thus you may multiply to infinity.*

J.Kerseboom pinxit.   B.Baron Sculp.

The Honourable ROBERT BOYLE.

After finishing "Praxis," Newton suddenly stopped in his tracks. The man who had been a workaholic all his life put down his pen and ceased his experiments. For the next eighteen months, he appears to have done almost no work on any subject. This is usually referred to as Newton's "nervous breakdown." Just what its cause was—whether clinical or psychological—is impossible to tell at this distance of time. There is little doubt, however, that Newton was hit by a deep bout of depression. He wrote strange, disjointed letters to some of his closest friends—including Pepys and Locke—accusing them of conspiring against him. He later retracted these accusations, saying he couldn't understand what had come over him. Perhaps he was temporarily insane.

Eventually Newton got back to business. He resumed his scientific work and his biblical studies. There is no evidence, however, that he ever resumed his alchemical research.

Is this, perhaps, a clue to the source of the problem? It seems suggestive, especially since Newton was so deeply involved in alchemical experiments immediately prior to his breakdown. Did something happen that convinced him alchemy was never going to work? Did he have a sudden insight into the "immense danger to the world" that worried him so much? Did he inadvertently poison himself with chemicals? Sadly, we will probably never know the truth of the matter.

Irish natural philosopher Robert Boyle was a mentor to Robert Hooke, a member of the Royal Society, and an alchemist.

Newton may have abandoned alchemy, but his interest in theology continued into old age. He became fascinated by the chronology of the ancient world, as revealed in the Bible and other historical texts. In 1716, soon after King George I ascended to the throne, Newton produced a long manuscript on the subject for the king's daughter-in-law, the future Queen Caroline. The document was meant for her eyes only, but an illicit copy found its way to France where it was published.

Newton was unhappy that his writing had been made public, and even more unhappy that the French subjected it to harsh criticism. He promptly penned a rebuttal of the criticisms and had it printed in 1725 as an open letter in the *Philosophical Transactions of the Royal Society*—one of the last works to be published during his lifetime.

Newton went back to his manuscript, revising it for official publication under the title *The Chronology of the Ancient Kingdoms Amended*. Although he finished it, he never lived to see it in print; the book appeared in 1728, the year after his death.

In retrospect, it is easy to see why the French were so critical of Newton's chronology. It differs in many ways from what was accepted at the time—and today, for that matter. Embarrassing as it sounds, Newton seems to have twisted the known facts in order to fit his pet theory—something he would never have dreamed of doing in his scientific work. But he had an obsession with the Temple of Solomon, partly, perhaps, because it is described in such mathematical detail in the Bible, and he wanted to give it a much earlier date than the one normally ascribed to it.

A second posthumous book, published in 1733, was entitled *Observations on the Prophecies of Daniel and the Apocalypse of St John.* This was Newton's attempt to connect biblical prophecies with subsequent historical events. Like his chronology, it contains very little that has stood the test of time. Newton himself may never have intended the book for publication; it may simply have been a way of cashing in on his name in the years immediately following his death.

For his supporters, Newton's religious books served another useful purpose, to show the world that he had been a profoundly religious person. His scientific theories, no matter how revolutionary they might seem, must therefore be entirely consistent with religious belief. At a time when atheists were viewed with fear and suspicion, this was a great help in securing Newton's posthumous reputation.

8 Making Money

Newton's visits to the Royal Society, and his brief stint in the House of Commons in 1689, gave him a taste for London life. The previous two decades—since the plague and the Great Fire—had seen a huge upsurge in the city's fortunes, and it now rivalled Paris and Amsterdam as the financial and cultural capital of Europe. Newton's correspondence shows that by the early 1690s he was growing tired of Cambridge. It is possible that the breakdown he suffered in 1693 owed

Isaac Newton became warden of the Royal Mint in 1969.

something to this feeling of dissatisfaction, or, then again, it may have contributed to it.

By 1695 Newton was actively looking for a new job. He was in his fifties now, and an increasing number of his peers had left Cambridge to take up comfortable and lucrative positions in public service. Newton resolved to do the same. He asked his friends to do whatever they could to secure a suitably prestigious post for him, preferably in London. To his dismay, the best anyone could offer was the mastership of Charterhouse School: a position out in the wilds of Surrey that offered no more in the way of remuneration than he was already earning at Cambridge. He turned the job down.

Eventually Newton's salvation came by way of the Chancellor of the Exchequer, Charles Montagu (1661–1715). Montagu had arrived at Trinity College as an eighteen-year-old student in 1679 and quickly formed a firm friendship with Newton. The friendship continued after Montagu graduated from university and embarked on a career in politics. He did well for himself; by 1694 he was chancellor to William III. During the reign of Queen Anne he fell out of favor somewhat, but when George I came to the throne in 1714 Montagu's fortunes rose again—though only briefly, since he died from lung problems the following year at the age of only fifty-four. In that last year of his life, he was made Earl of Halifax and First Lord of the Treasury.

From Newton's point of view, Montagu's rise meant he had a friend in high places. This proved to be every bit as profitable

Charles Montagu befriended Newton when they were at Trinity College together. Montagu would later become Earl of Halifax and help to advance Newton's career.

for him as he might have hoped. In 1696, soon after Montagu became chancellor, he succeeded in getting Newton appointed to one of the most lucrative civil service positions in the country, as warden of the Royal Mint. Newton promptly left Cambridge, having lived there for thirty-five years, with no indication that he ever looked back. He retained his college fellowship and university chair, but in title only. From that point on, his life lay in London. For the first few months he lodged at the mint itself, inside the Tower of London, before moving to a more comfortable house on Jermyn Street, St James's.

Newton's friendship with Montagu had an unexpected benefit. In 1705, during the reign of Queen Anne, Montagu was trying as hard as he could to reestablish his political career. Part of his plan was to get a few more of his supporters into the House of Commons. To this end, he wanted Newton to stand for Parliament again. To give him a better chance of success, Montagu put Newton's name forward for a knighthood. The queen, who was a great admirer of Newton, conferred the honor on him with pleasure. Newton failed to be elected to Parliament, but at least he got the knighthood—not in recognition of his scientific achievements or his work at the mint, but simply as a side effect of Montagu's political ambitions!

Soon after Newton had settled into the house on Jermyn Street, he was joined by a lively teenage girl named Catherine Barton (1679–1739). She was his niece, a daughter of one of the half sisters he had acquired as a result of his mother's second marriage. He hadn't been too happy about those half siblings at the time, but—now in his mid-fifties—he was only too pleased to have Catherine around to look after the house for him.

Catherine remained with Newton for the rest of his life— even after her marriage in 1717 to a civil servant named John

Conduitt (1688–1737), the man who took over from Newton at the mint. There was genuine mutual affection between Newton and Catherine, who seems to have been the only female who played a significant role in his adult life. There are no records of any romantic liaisons, and one of the reasons for Newton's temporary falling out with Pepys and Locke in 1693 was his—almost certainly erroneous—belief that they "endeavoured to embroil me with women."

Catherine was very different from her uncle. No one ever accused Newton of being the life and soul of the party. By contrast, Catherine grew into a gregarious, witty, and intelligent woman who became the talk of London society. One acquaintance on whom she made a particularly strong impression was the Irish writer and satirist Jonathan Swift (1667–1745), best known as the author of *Gulliver's Travels*. Between the years 1710 and 1711, Swift dined with Catherine at her home on several occasions, which he recorded with enthusiasm in his *Journal to Stella*. At no point, however, does he bother to mention that Sir Isaac Newton—one of the most famous men in London—happened to live in the same house!

Catherine was thirty-eight when she married Conduitt, quite an advanced age for a first marriage in the eighteenth century. Why did she wait so long? A clue may lie in the fact that Newton's influential friend, Charles Montagu—by that time the Earl of Halifax—had died just two years earlier, in 1715. In his will, the earl left Catherine £5,000, together with all his jewels—an astonishingly generous bequest. Not surprisingly, a few eyebrows were raised. John Flamsteed offered the facetious suggestion that Lord Halifax had left her the money "for her excellent conversation." No one has ever managed to prove that Catherine and Montagu were lovers, but the circumstantial evidence certainly points in that direction.

Catherine's inheritance of £5,000 may not sound much by today's standards, but money went much farther three centuries ago. The purchasing power of £5,000 in 1715 to pounds in 2014 is about £698,200, which converts to about US $993,189 —a small fortune indeed.

There are other ways in which money has changed over the years, besides the simple matter of spending power. Today, we think of it as a variable asset that can rise or fall in value with the vagaries of the economy. For the most part, "money" in the modern world isn't even a tangible thing—simply numbers in a computer that record the status of one's bank account.

When Newton took over the running of the Royal Mint in 1696, the situation was very different. Concepts such as paper money, bank accounts, and credit were only just emerging. The Bank of England had been founded just two years earlier, in 1694, and for the first time in English history banknotes had been issued in lieu of coins. To most people, "money" was still synonymous with "coinage." Coins were more than tokens. They were made of silver or gold, and their intrinsic value as a precious metal was—in theory at least—precisely equal to their face value.

The Charles II half crown was made of silver.

At a time when money meant coinage, the Royal Mint was the country's foremost financial establishment. The warden of the Mint—the man responsible for its day-to-day running—was one of the most powerful public servants in the country. As of May 1696, that man was Isaac Newton.

As soon as he arrived, Newton discovered he had a national crisis on his hands—a currency instability that was threatening to engulf England's money supply. The problem boiled down to the fact that there were two different types of silver coin in circulation. Old coins, dating from before the time of Charles II, were hand-made and lacked milled edges. That meant it was a simple matter for unscrupulous individuals to clip bits of metal from around the edges and make themselves instantly richer in the process. They would still have the same coin, with the same face value, but now they also had some flakes of pure silver. The old coins had another weakness, too. They were relatively easy to counterfeit, using cheaper metal. Like a clipped coin, a counterfeit coin had an intrinsic value that was substantially lower than its face value.

More recent, machine-made coins, on the other hand, were harder to counterfeit because of their more intricate design, and they were almost impossible to clip because of their milled edges. Unlike the older coins, their intrinsic value never fell below face value. This dichotomy had an inevitable consequence. People soon learned to spend the old, lower-value coins and hoard the new, higher-value coins. The result was a downward spiral in money supply, with the total value of coins in circulation steadily getting lower and lower.

England was experiencing the ill effects of the well-known economic principle that "bad money drives out good." This is usually referred to as Gresham's law, after the Elizabethan financier Thomas Gresham (1519–1579), but much the same principle had been put forward a quarter of a century earlier by an obscure cathedral administrator in northern Poland. His name was Nicolaus Copernicus—the same Copernicus who went on to propose the sun-centered model of the planetary system that ultimately sparked Newton's work on gravity. By a neat coincidence, it was the "bad money drives out good" theory—also due to Copernicus—that paved the way for Newton's work at the Royal Mint.

Even before Newton arrived in London, the government had decided the only way to resolve the crisis was to undertake a massive recoinage project. Every single coin would be removed from circulation and melted down. New coins would be minted, using the latest machinery, to a precise specification that would minimize the risk of clipping and counterfeiting.

It was an excellent idea in principle, but putting principle into practice was proving harder than expected. The project was a shambles. By the time Newton took up his post, he found the mint in chaos. The machinery was completely inadequate to the scale of the task. Production was already months behind schedule and falling farther behind as each day passed. Old coins had been withdrawn from circulation too quickly, before there were enough new coins to replace them. Put simply, England was running dangerously short of cash.

"The people are discontented to the utmost; many self-murders happen in small families for want […] Should the least accident put the mob in motion no man can tell where it would end." Those words were written in July 1696 by the political activist Edmund Bohun (1645–1699). He was not exaggerating. Starved of cash, the country was lurching towards crisis—possibly even anarchy or revolution. The ultimate source of the problem was the Royal Mint—more specifically, its culture of poor management. Previous wardens simply hadn't taken their job sufficiently seriously. The new warden, however, was going to be very different. Newton took *everything* seriously. He took natural philosophy seriously. He took mathematics and theology and alchemy seriously. And he was going to take his role at the Royal Mint seriously. As Keynes observed, "He became one of the greatest and most efficient of our civil servants."

Within months, Newton had revolutionized the working of the mint. He kept careful track of expenses to reduce costs. He measured everything: the amount of raw material consumed, the number of men and horses involved, the time taken by various processes. He identified weak points and bottlenecks and focused his attention on those. He installed additional furnaces and new rolling mills and coining presses. Eventually he increased productivity from 15,000 pounds (6.8 metric tons) of silver per week to 100,000 pounds (45.4 t). The recoinage project was no longer behind schedule—it was *ahead* of schedule.

The entire enterprise was completed by the middle of 1698, a mere two years after Newton's arrival at the mint. Once again, all the country's silver—6.8 million pounds (3084.4 t) of it—was circulating from person to person in the form of coins. Isaac Newton had given the country its money back.

The new coins put the clippers out of business once and for all. The milled design made it impossible to scrape off even the tiniest amount of silver without being detected. Counterfeiting, however, remained a problem. As soon as the new coins hit the streets, they were joined by counterfeits made of cheap metal. Some of these were more convincing than others. The new design was intricate and precise, but the most skilled counterfeiters soon found a way of duplicating it. And even the crudest counterfeits could sometimes pass for the real thing in a dimly lit tavern.

The person with ultimate responsibility for enforcing the law against counterfeiting, and all other forms of currency crime, was the warden of the Mint. It was an aspect of the job Newton pursued as assiduously as any other. First, he had himself sworn in as a justice of the peace in all the surrounding counties to make it easier for him to pursue suspects and take statements from witnesses. Next, he built up a network of undercover agents and criminal informers, even going undercover himself when necessary. In October 1699 the treasury received a bill from the warden of the Mint to the sum of £120 (US$21,324 in 2014) for "various small expenses in coach-hire and at taverns and prisons and other places." It appears Newton was not above bribing witnesses in order to get the information he needed!

It would be natural to think that Newton, the epitome of the rational scientist, went about his detective work in the cool, dispassionate style of a Sherlock Holmes. There is little doubt, however, that he developed a visceral hatred for the criminals he pursued; one writer has even referred to him as "17th-Century London's Dirty Harry"! In total, Newton secured the successful prosecution of twenty-eight counterfeiters, many of whom were promptly sent to the gallows. Interfering with His Majesty's coinage was punishable by death—an entirely fitting outcome, as far as Newton was concerned. To him, producing counterfeit money was nothing short of treason. He had witnessed at first hand its destabilizing effect on the national economy.

Newton's most formidable opponent was a man named William Chaloner. He was the leader of a counterfeiting ring that had been growing in size and profitability since 1691. Chaloner was a skilled counterfeiter. He was also an audacious conman, prepared to pit his wits against the government itself. Even before Newton arrived at the mint, Chaloner had started a propaganda offensive. He made bold accusations of a criminal conspiracy that, he claimed, extended to within the very walls of the mint itself. He wrote pamphlets on the subject and lobbied members of Parliament. He even made a personal appeal to the Chancellor of the Exchequer—Newton's friend Charles Montagu. When a set of dies—specialist tools used in coin-making—disappeared from the mint early in 1696, Montagu decided there was sufficient cause to hold an official investigation into Chaloner's allegations.

Chaloner informed the ensuing Parliamentary committee that the set of dies had been stolen by a senior mint official, who had then sold them on to counterfeiters. Other witnesses testified that

Chaloner himself was the leader of the counterfeiting ring that ended up with the stolen dies. Yet a third affidavit maintained that the mint's officials were innocent and that the theft of the dies had been the work of Chaloner's own men. This last version of events turned out to be the correct one—although several years were to pass before anything could be proved beyond doubt.

Prosecuting high-level counterfeiters was notoriously difficult. Low-ranking henchmen would happily incriminate more or less anyone if it meant saving themselves from the gallows. Juries were well aware of this, so they rarely paid attention to uncorroborated witness testimony—it was too likely to be perjured. As a result, it was almost impossible to bring a successful case against a master criminal like William Chaloner.

Audacious as his crimes were, Chaloner might have remained a free man but for one thing. The new warden of the Mint, Isaac Newton, was on his track. Using his network of informers and agents, Newton doggedly built up his case—physical evidence, witness statements, names, dates, and places—until he was certain it was one that no jury could ignore. Even the supremely arrogant Chaloner seems to have realized he had finally met his match. He tried to buy off the jury, and when that failed he tried feigning madness. But that didn't work either. At his trial at the Old Bailey on March 3, 1699, every shred of evidence Newton had collected was thrown at him. There was only one possible verdict: guilty. And only one possible sentence: death. It probably made Newton's day.

In December of the same year, 1699, Newton was promoted to master of the mint. This was essentially a figurehead position, with far fewer day-to-day duties than that of warden, but with more generous remuneration. Newton became one of the highest paid public servants in the country, with an annual income averaging over £2,000 (about $355,452 US in 2014).

The financial stability created by the recoinage project did not last. In the early years of the eighteenth century the country was threatened with a fresh monetary crisis. It gradually became apparent that the new silver coins were slowly but steadily disappearing from circulation. Newton quickly discovered the cause: coins were being sold abroad—to Europe first, and from there onto India and China—where their exchange value as silver was worth more than their face value in England. In other words, English silver was being used to buy foreign gold.

The root of the problem was the requirement that coins should have a face value equal to their intrinsic metallic value. So why not replace them with cheap tokens, made of something far less valuable than silver or gold? Why not use paper money? Why not allow the value of a currency to float up and down, in order to accommodate fluctuations in international markets? Such ideas may seem obvious today, but they were far from apparent at the start of the eighteenth century. Most people felt that money should be worth the exact figure that was stamped on it. Only a small minority dared to disagree with this view. Newton, ahead of his time here, as in so many other ways, was among this latter group: "It is mere opinion that sets a value upon money. We value it because we can purchase all sorts of commodities and the same opinion sets a like value upon paper security."

Ironically, having saved the country from economic ruin on more than one occasion, Newton suffered a financial disaster of his own in his old age. Over a period of several years he bought shares in the South Sea Company, happily watching them grow in value from £128 (about $24,000 US in 2014) per share to a peak of £1,050 ($200,000 US) in June 1720. Newton, like any over-enthusiastic investor, continued to buy more and more shares as the price rose. Then the bubble burst. The share price plummeted back to £175 (about $33,000 US in 2014) in just three months, and Newton lost more than £20,000 (more than $3.8 million US) in the process. With hindsight, the disaster was inevitable. The South Sea bubble was in essence a pyramid scheme and thus doomed on basic mathematical grounds. Newton—one of the greatest mathematicians who ever lived—only realized this when it was too late. He complained bitterly to a friend that he "could not calculate the madness of the people."

Newton did not lose everything in the South Sea debacle, however. When he died a few years later, he left an estate of £31,821—more than $6 million US in today's money. Since he had no immediate heirs, the estate was divided equally between eight half nephews and half nieces. Among the beneficiaries was Catherine Conduitt—who thus received a substantial inheritance for the second time in her life.

9 Death and Apotheosis

As Newton entered his eighties, his health began to fail. In 1726, at the age of eighty-three, he was forced to move out of central London to the fresher atmosphere of Kensington, which was then little more than a country village. But the respite it gave him was temporary. On March 20, 1727, old age finally took its toll and Newton died—less than three weeks after presiding at his last meeting of the Royal Society.

The monument to Sir Isaac Newton in Westminster Abbey honors him for his scientific achievements.

Newton's death shocked the country; he had become a national institution. For a week prior to his funeral, his body lay in state in Westminster Abbey—an honor granted to few commoners—before being interred there with every ceremony. The funeral procession included the Lord High Chancellor, two dukes, and three earls. The proceedings were observed first hand by the French philosopher Voltaire, who had recently arrived in London after being exiled from his own country. He was astonished and impressed by the fact that Newton, a mere academic, was "buried like a king who has done well by his subjects."

Voltaire became one of the key figures of the European Enlightenment, and he, as much as anyone, raised Newton to the posthumous status of a demigod. He wrote a popularization of Newton's work called *Éléments de la philosophie de Newton*, "Elements of the Philosophy of Newton," in 1738. The book helped to ensure that Newton's ideas on gravity, mechanics, and optics became as firmly established on the Continent as they already were in the English-speaking world.

No one succeeded in expressing Newton's achievement better than the poet Alexander Pope. He produced the following epitaph in the form of a heroic couplet:

> *Nature and Nature's laws lay hid in night:*
> *God said, Let Newton be! and all was light.*

Pope wanted to see these words carved on Newton's tomb in Westminster Abbey. Perhaps not surprisingly, the church authorities decided they would prefer something displaying a little more humility!

The eventual inscription is in Latin. Translated into English, it reads:

> *Diligent, sagacious and faithful in his expositions of nature, antiquity and the holy Scriptures, he vindicated by his philosophy the majesty of God mighty and good, and expressed the simplicity of the Gospel in his manners. Mortals rejoice that there has existed such and so great an ornament of the human race!*

It is interesting that the official inscription gives equal billing to Newton's work in science and theology. The first of these is as valid today as it was in his own time, while the second is all but forgotten. Does that mean, as some biographers have suggested, that Newton's nonscientific work was pointless and irrelevant—a waste of intellectual effort?

The mistake is to suppose that it is possible to separate Newton's achievement from the sum total of his personality. The latter was complex and multifaceted, and all those components were active in everything he did. The mystical dreamer studying alchemical texts was also the scientific rationalist working out the mathematics of gravity. Newton was one man with a multitude of talents.

- Mathematical brilliance. Newton was one of the greatest mathematicians of his time. He invented calculus and was brilliant at computation. But Newton's mathematics had more to do with algebraic symbols and geometric patterns than it did with numbers alone.
- Pattern-matching imagination. An obsession with patterns and symbols also lies at the heart of his fascination with alchemy and the mysteries of Hermetic philosophy: "As above, so below." By his middle years he had developed a near-mystical belief in the interconnectedness of the material and spiritual worlds.
- Rigorous determination. Newton was a seeker after truth. He was convinced there was a hidden order underpinning the universe—a conviction that motivated his theological speculations every bit as much as it did his scientific work.
- Practical ingenuity. Newton was a problem solver. That was evident in the gadget-building of his teenage years, and it led to the construction of the world's first reflecting telescope. It almost certainly saved the country from financial disaster when he took over the running of the Royal Mint.

The *Principia* could only have been written by someone who was at one and the same time a mathematician, a mystic, a truth seeker, and a problem solver. It is pointless to suggest that Newton would have achieved more had he not wasted his time on alchemy and theology. He would not have achieved anything at all.

Like most biographies of Newton, this book has focused almost exclusively on his work—because, of course, that is what makes him a giant. Unfortunately, such an approach can make him seem more one-dimensional than he actually was. Yes, he was an absent-minded workaholic. And yes, he had violent arguments with Hooke, Leibniz, and Flamsteed. But he also had many close friends, such as Halley, Locke, and Montagu. He had other friends, too, who are less likely to feature in a story of his life because they had no connection with his work. One such was William Stukeley (1687–1765), a pioneer of archaeology who produced the first full-length biography of Newton. This features Stukeley's first-hand recollections of Newton's later life, including this scene:

> *Sir Isaac enjoyed himself extremely in this society of his countrymen; and talked much, and pleasantly. Particularly I remember one part of the conversation turned upon music, of which Sir Isaac was fond; and of the operas then beginning to be in vogue among us. It was no wonder his soul should be delighted with harmony. Sir Isaac said they were very fine entertainments; but that*

English archivist William Stukeley wrote the first full-length biography of Isaac Newton's life.

"there was too much of a good thing; it was like a surfeit at dinner. I went to the last opera." says he. "The first act gave me the greatest pleasure. The second quite tired me: at the third I ran away."

In recent years a number of writers have tried to put Sir Isaac on the psychiatrist's couch. It has been suggested that he was homosexual because he showed no interest in women and spent thirty years of his life in an all-male college. Or maybe he suffered from Asperger syndrome because he lived in a fantasy world (he believed in alchemy) and lacked empathy (he was in favor of the death penalty). While such theories undoubtedly sell books—and may even seem convincing to some—closer analysis suggests they have more to do with the different social norms of Newton's time than with the man himself.

There are several portraits of Newton in existence, most of them dating from his later years in London. One of the best known, however, was painted by Sir Godfrey Kneller (1646–1723) in 1689, just two years after the publication of the *Principia*, while Newton was still living in Cambridge. To the modern eye, it is the most "photographic" of all the portraits, showing a serious-faced Newton—looking younger than his forty-seven years—with a prominent chin, nose and brows. The same facial features can be seen in the death-mask made thirty-eight years later. By this time Newton had put on some weight, but otherwise looks more like a man of sixty-five than eighty-five. Recalling Newton in his old age, John Conduitt wrote:

He was blessed with a very happy and vigorous constitution, he was of a middle stature and plump in his later years, had a very lively and piercing eye and a comely and gracious aspect; had a fine head of hair as white as silver without any baldness and when his periwig was off was a venerable sight, and to his last illness had the bloom and colour of a young man and never used spectacles nor lost any more than one tooth to the day of his death.

During the eighteenth and nineteenth centuries, Newton's name became as much a byword for genius as Einstein's is today. His laws of gravity and motion were still at the cutting edge of science more than a century after he wrote the *Principia*. Over time, there were refinements to his work, inevitably. While Newton's basic theory appeared unassailable, his mathematical techniques were rather clumsy by later standards. An alternative, less unwieldy, mathematical formulation of Newton's theory was put forward by the French astronomer Laplace. His *Mécanique Céleste*, "Celestial Mechanics," was published in five volumes between 1799 and 1825.

On one point at least Laplace used Newton's own theory to outdo Newton himself. The Frenchman proved that the solar

Isaac Newton's death mask on display with a handwritten copy of *Principia*

LAPLACE.

French astronomer Pierre-Simon Laplace expanded on
Newton's mathematical techniques and astronomical theories.

system was dynamically stable in the long term. Newton had believed the system was inherently unstable, and that it relied on occasional interventions by God to prevent it falling apart. This became one of Newton's better-known results. Although it was hardly "scientific proof of the existence of God," it certainly hinted at the compatibility of science and religion. But Laplace changed all that. According to a famous anecdote, the emperor Napoleon once asked him about the subject. Laplace replied, in no uncertain terms: "Sir, I have no need of that hypothesis."

In the history of physics, Laplace represents the pinnacle of the purely Newtonian world view. During the course of the nineteenth century, the focus of interest began to shift. New subdisciplines emerged, such as electromagnetism and thermodynamics. Yet even these proved amenable to the basic approach that Newton had pioneered. Electromagnetic and thermodynamic properties could be represented by mathematical symbols, and the interactions between them could be described using mathematical equations. Although it had long since been forgotten, the old Hermetic adage was still true: "As above, so below."

It remained true even with the emergence of quantum theory and **relativity** in the twentieth century. These are complex and profoundly counterintuitive subjects, yet they can be described by mathematics as completely and precisely as anything in the *Principia*.

Even as the world moves forward, Newton's legacy lives on. In 1948, the international unit of force—equal to 1 kilogram force (meter per second squared)—was named the "newton" in his honor. There is a Newton crater on the moon and another on Mars. There is an asteroid named 8000 Isaac Newton and another named 2653 Principia. The Isaac Newton Telescope, on the island of La Palma in the Atlantic Ocean, is one of the most powerful ground-based optical telescopes in the world. (In terms of its basic design, it is not really that different from the tiny reflecting telescope Newton built himself in 1668.)

Newton's work at the Royal Mint has been commemorated, too. For ten years, between 1978 and 1988, his portrait was featured on every pound note issued by the Bank of England. Later, his famous words to Robert Hooke—"Standing on the Shoulders of Giants"—were stamped around the edge of the two-pound coin.

In the piazza of the British Library in London, there is a huge bronze statue of Newton, produced by Eduardo Paolozzi after an eighteenth-century print by William Blake. More recently, Newton—or at any rate, fanciful speculation about Newton—has played a major role in the plots of two of Dan Brown's best-selling novels, *The Da Vinci Code* and *The Lost Symbol*.

The most important homage to Newton's memory, of course, is the fact that so many people still draw on his scientific discoveries in their everyday work. All around the world, countless scientists and engineers make routine use of those mathematical principles of natural philosophy that were first articulated in *Philosophiae*

One of the most powerful telescopes in the world, located on the Canary Islands, is named for Isaac Newton.

On February 9, 1978, the £1 note with Isaac Newton on the reverse was released. He is pictured with the heliocentric solar system, his telescope, a prism, and the *Prinicpia*.

Naturalis Principia Mathematica. From cars to fighter jets, from cruise ships to satellites, modern engineering simply would not be possible without Newton's laws. When a spacecraft touches down on the surface of Mars, in the exact spot and at the exact second it is supposed to, that is because of Isaac Newton.

Chronology

1642 December 25, born at Woolsthorpe Manor

1654 Attends the King's School, Grantham

1661 Enters Cambridge as an undergraduate at Trinity College

1665 Graduates, then returns to Woolsthorpe when plague breaks out

1667 Returns to Trinity, where he becomes a fellow

1669 Appointed Lucasian Professor of Mathematics

1671 Demonstrates his reflecting telescope to the Royal Society

1672 Elected a fellow of the Royal Society

1675 Charles II frees the Lucasian Professor from the obligation to take holy orders

1684 Halley asks Newton to write up his theory of orbits

1687 *Philosophiae Naturalis Principia Mathematica* published by the Royal Society

1689 Represents Cambridge University in the Convention Parliament

1693 Descends into depression, possibly due to failed alchemical experiments

1696 Becomes warden of the Royal Mint in London

1698 Completion of the recoinage project

1699 Prosecution of Chaloner for counterfeiting

1700 Promoted to master of the mint

1701 Elected to his second short stint as MP for Cambridge University

1703 Elected president of the Royal Society

1704 Second major book, *Opticks*, is published

1705 Knighted by Queen Anne

1713 Revised edition of the *Principia*

1720 Loses more than £20,000 (more than $3.8 million US in 2014) in the South Sea bubble

1727 March 20, dies at home in Kensington

Dates are given according to the Julian calendar in use in England at the time. (Confusingly the year of death is sometimes given as 1726 because the Julian year officially clicked over on March 25 instead of January 1!)

Glossary

alchemy A practice originating in prescientific times, with various goals, including the transmutation of base metals into gold. The study of alchemy combines practical experimentation with mystical philosophy.

analogous Showing a likeness or being related to.

applied mathematics The study of mathematics as it is applied to other disciplines such as physics or engineering; the abstract science of number, quantity, and space.

Aristotelian Philosophy or methodology from or relating to the Greek philosopher Aristotle.

binomial theorem In algebra, a binomial is the sum of two terms. The binomial theorem, in its original form, was a formula by which a binomial could be raised to the power of a positive whole number. Newton generalized this formula so that the power could be a negative or fractional number.

calculus A branch of mathematics that analyzes complex shapes and motions by breaking them down into infinitesimally small pieces. It is the primary mathematical technique used in theoretical physics and engineering.

centrifugal Moving away from a center or in a direction away from a center axis.

ellipse A type of oval that, according to Kepler's third law, is the generic shape of a planetary orbit.

fluxion Flowing or changing action or something subjected to it; the method of fluxions is differential calculus.

Hermetic Related to the mystical and alchemical writings and teachings of Hermes Trismegistus in the first three centuries CE; also refers to occultism.

Hermetica Ancient texts, couched in obscure symbolic language, that seek to explain the nature of life and the cosmos. A central element of the Hermetica is the doctrine "as above, so below."

inverse square A relationship whereby a quantity, such as the force of gravity, diminishes in inverse proportion to the square of the distance. To give an example: if the distance is doubled, the force is reduced to a quarter of its original value.

law of gravity A mathematical relationship describing the magnitude of the force between any two bodies. It is proportional to the mass of each body and to the inverse square of the distance between them.

natural philosophy Prior to the use of the word "science," meaning natural science, especially physical.

Newtonian The doctrines or theories related to Isaac Newton, particularly pertaining to his work in physical science: gravity, optics, mechanics, and the scientific method.

occult Relating to supernatural powers or practices; literally meaning hidden from view or concealed.

optics The study of light and vision. In Newton's time, optics was principally concerned with the way light behaves when it encounters a glass prism, lens, or mirror.

point mass A mathematical convenience used in the theory of orbits. A point mass exerts a gravitational force, like a planet, but unlike a planet its volume can be ignored.

quantum theory A branch of physics originating in the twentieth century that deals with energy and matter on extremely small scales. Contrary to some popular accounts, it is a rigorously mathematical discipline.

relativity A twentieth-century development, due primarily to Albert Einstein, providing a new description of physics at extremely high speeds and in very strong gravitational fields. Nevertheless, Newton's laws remain completely valid in the everyday world.

scientific method The systematic pursuit of knowledge beginning with the identification or formulation of a problem, followed by the collection of data through observation and/or experimentation, with the goal of forming and testing a hypothesis.

theory of vortices Theorized by René Descartes, the idea that space is filled with matter all swirling around the sun and that particle collisions pushed matter toward it. Though disproven, this theory influenced scientific theory and hypothesis in the seventeenth century.

Further Information

Books

Ackroyd, Peter. *Newton*. New York, NY: Vintage Books, 2007.

Asimov, Isaac. *Biographical Encyclopedia of Science and Technology*. London, England: Pan Books, 1975.

Benson, Donald C. *The Ballet of the Planets: On the Mathematical Elegance of Planetary Motion*. New York, NY: Oxford University Press, 2012.

Clegg, B. *Gravity: Why What Goes Up, Must Come Down*. London, England: Duckworth Overlook, 2012.

Levenson, Thomas. *Newton and the Counterfeiter*. London, England: Faber and Faber, 2009.

Picknett, Lynn, and Clive Prince. *The Forbidden Universe.* London, England: Constable, 2011.

Westfall, Richard S. *Isaac Newton*. New York, NY: Oxford University Press, 2007.

Websites

A Complicated Man

www.pbs.org/wgbh/nova/physics/complicated-man.html

Dr. Jed Buchwald, a historian of physics and professor of history at the California Institute of Technology, answers questions about Isaac Newton. The interview-style article talks about Newton's genius and personality.

Isaac Newton Biography

www.biography.com/people/isaac-newton-9422656

The Bio page on Isaac Newton includes a comprehensive article about his personal and professional life, quick facts, and quotations. Several videos discuss his vital accomplishments to science.

The Mind of Isaac Newton

cll.mcmaster.ca/multimedia_projects/sample/newton/home.htm

Breaking down Newton into his aspects as a mathematician, visionary, and physicist, this page has videos and animations about Newton and his scientific theories and projects. Further resources include timelines, a synopsis of Newton's *Principia*, and additional resources.

Bibliography

Andrade, Edward Neville da Costa. *Sir Isaac Newton*. London, England: Fontana Books, 1961.

Charon, J. *Cosmology: Theories of the Universe*. London, England: Weidenfeld and Nicolson, 1970.

Clegg, B. *Gravity: Why What Goes Up, Must Come Down*. London, England: Duckworth Overlook, 2012.

Conduitt, John. "Fair Copy of the Memoir of Newton," 1727. The Newton Project. http://www.newtonproject.sussex.ac.uk/view/texts/normalized/THEM00145.

Dutton, Judy. "Isaac Newton: 17th-Century London's Dirty Harry." Mental Floss. http://mentalfloss.com/article/13035/isaac-newton-17th-century-london%E2%80%99s-dirty-harry.

Gleick, James. *Isaac Newton*. London, England: Fourth Estate, 2003.

Keynes, John Maynard. "Newton, the Man." http://www-history.mcs.st-and.ac.uk/Extras/Keynes_Newton.html.

Levenson, Thomas. *Newton and the Counterfeiter*. London, England: Faber and Faber, 2009.

Maury, J. P. *Newton: Understanding the Cosmos*. London, England: Thames and Hudson, 1992.

Picknett, Lynn, and Clive Prince. *The Forbidden Universe*. London, England: Constable, 2011.

Snobelen, Stephen D. "'A Time and Times and the Dividing of Time': Isaac Newton, the Apocalypse, and 2060 A.D." December 2003. https://isaacnewtonstheology.files.wordpress.com/2013/06/newton-the-apocalypse-and-2060-ad.pdf.

Stukeley, William. "Memoirs of Sir Isaac Newton's Life," 1752. The Newton Project. http://www.newtonproject.sussex.ac.uk/view/texts/normalized/OTHE00001.

Westfall, Richard S. *Isaac Newton*. New York, NY: Oxford University Press, 2007.

White, Michael. *Isaac Newton: The Last Sorcerer*. London, England: Fourth Estate, 1997.

Index

Page numbers in **boldface** are illustrations. Entries in **boldface** are glossary terms.